To
Tony Barnhart
A great friend and
asset to Green-Coun...
and College Football

[signature]

With best wishes,
[signature] Hal Winlton

Advance Commentary for *Policing Greene*

"Law enforcement has become a different profession over the last decade, which, to tell the truth, makes me wish for the "Good Ole Days" and for my old friend, Mr. Carlton Lewis. Chief Lewis did everything in his life in an honest, worthy, and upstanding manner, especially his job as Police Chief for the City of Union Point, GA.

"At 7 am, you would see the Chief walking downtown to Rhodes Drug Store. He would sit with all "the regulars" and catch up on the news and learn where to begin his daily duties. By 10 am Chief Lewis would be knocking on doors to check on the residents of his city and make sure all was well. At noon, he would be walking home to Woodland Court to have lunch with his devoted wife, Eleanor.

"The afternoon schedule would hold many duties for our police. You see, Chief Lewis was our police department from A to Z. He did it all in a protective and reassuring way. Things were not always just a quiet daily routine, and when they were not Chief Lewis handled the situation in stride. One of our worst homicides in history happened in Union Point while Chief Lewis was in charge. The case was handled professionally and justice was served!

"Chief Lewis never punched a time clock, and he never said, '"This is not in my job description.' He always did whatever necessary to protect Union Point and get the job done.

"When 5 pm rolled around, you would see Chief Lewis walking home for supper. After eating and a short rest, he would be back in town, sitting at the filling station with the crowd and putting Union Point to bed.

"No other policeman, chief, or human being could ever be our Mr. Carlton Lewis. He was my friend and truly one of a kind!

"*Policing Greene* is a welcome and finely-written depiction of this wonderful man."

— Lanier Rhodes, Mayor
Union Point, Georgia

✛ ✛ ✛ ✛

"Carlton Lewis was and is an icon of Union Point. Everyone knew and loved him. He loved his job, the people, and Union Point. He walked to work every day to serve and do his job, and shook every business door before heading home. Most of us living there weren't aware of the many dangerous situations he handled on our behalf, while giving out bubble gum to any child he saw! This terrific book at last tells his wonderful story."

— Trey Rhodes, State Representative
& Governor's Floor Leader
Georgia House of Representatives
Greensboro, Georgia

"Carlton Lewis was a one-of-a-kind police officer who was respected by all walks of life. He was a hard-working policeman who was on the job from daylight to dawn. He could handle himself and if some law breaker wanted to fight, he could mix it up with them with the certain result of their arrest. He loved his job, his town, and the people he served, and he dedicated his life to that service. Hal McAlister has captured all these aspects of this fine man's life in a page-turner of a book."

— Carey Williams, Publisher & Editor
The Herald-Journal
Greensboro, Georgia

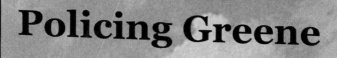

Policing Greene

A Policeman at the Sunset
of the Jim Crow South

by

HAROLD A. McALISTER

in collaboration with

THOMAS C. LEWIS

Cover and layout by the author

ISBN 978-1-98339-492-8

First Edition, 2018

Cover photographs are from the Library of Congress, Prints and Photographs Division, under the subject heading "Union Point, Georgia." These public domain images were taken by Jack Delano for the U.S. Farm Security Administration Office of War Information in the summer and fall of 1941. Top half-page image shows a scene "along the road from Union Point to Woodville" LC-USF34- 046350-D. Bottom half images, clockwise from upper left: "Union Point, Georgia," showing Farmers Bank on Sibley Avenue LC-USF34-044636-D; "Saturday afternoon in Union Point" with three men in front of Rhodes drug store LC-USF33-020950-M4; the "second shift at the textile mill in Union Point" LC-USF33-020959-M2; and "Saturday afternoon outside a Negro store and barbershop in Union Point" LC-USF33- 020957-M2. Inset is a photo, copyrighted by Thomas C. Lewis, of Carlton Lewis, Chief of Police of Union Point, Georgia, 1973-1986.

"People sleep peaceably in their beds at night only because rough men stand ready to do violence on their behalf."

— George Orwell

"Most middle-class whites have no idea what it feels like to be subjected to police who are routinely suspicious, rude, belligerent, and brutal."

— Benjamin Spock

"As you grow older, you'll see white men cheat black men every day of your life, but let me tell you something and don't you forget it—whenever a white man does that to a black man, no matter who he is, how rich he is, or how fine a family he comes from, that white man is trash"

— Harper Lee in *To Kill a Mockingbird*

"I speak to everyone in the same way, whether he is the garbage man or the president of the university."

— Albert Einstein

"When all is said and done, the one sole condition that makes spiritual happiness and preserves it is the absence of doubt."

— Mark Twain in *Eruption*

"Go ahead. Make my day."

— Clint Eastwood as Harry Hallahan in *Sudden Impact*

"As a Southerner born after the epic events of the civil rights movement, I've always wondered how on earth people of good will could have conceivably lived with Jim Crow - with the daily degradations, the lynchings in plain sight, and, as the movement gathered force, with the fire hoses and the police dogs and the billy clubs."

— Jon Meacham

"All you gotta do is tell them you're going to bring the dogs. Look at em run. I want to see the dogs work."

— Bull Conner

"The civil rights movement should thank God for Bull Connor. He helped it as much as Abraham Lincoln."

— John F. Kennedy

"You never know how a horse will pull until you hook him to a heavy load."

— Bear Bryant

"To make a good policeman, you've got to love people; you've got to want to help people."

— Carlton Lewis

"Blessed is the man who remains steadfast under trial, for when he has stood the test he will receive the crown of life, which God has promised to those who love him."

— James 1:1

Table of Contents

Foreword

I had the pleasure of meeting Chief Carlton Lewis in 1982 when I was introduced to him by his son, Tom Lewis, while he was serving as President of the Cartersville-Bartow County Chamber of Commerce. Tom became very active in my campaign for Governor and joined my staff rising to Chief of Staff.

Chief Lewis was a dedicated policeman who loved people and hated crime. I was most impressed with his strong faith and his desire to treat everyone equally and with respect. I appointed Chief Lewis to the Georgia Criminal Justice Coordinating Council where he served our state faithfully until his death.

Policing Greene written by Dr. Hal McAlister is an excellent account of how policing should be done. Chief Lewis was a people person, and he always let his actions be guided by his deep religious beliefs and his love for his family and his community.

— Joe Frank Harris
Former Governor of Georgia
Cartersville, Georgia

Tom Lewis, Carlton Lewis and Governor Joe Frank Harris at the Georgia Capitol in 1985.

Preface

As I grow older, I find that I am much more appreciative and nostalgic about the years I spent growing up in Union Point, Georgia. It was a small, close-knit community where people knew me and my parents and genuinely cared about me and supported me in any way they could. Sometimes this involved ratting me out to my mother and my father – a teacher and a policeman – but only to protect me from the perils of youth. Many of the Union Point folks were instrumental in shaping and preparing me for life as an adult.

My Dad began his law enforcement career as I was beginning my high school experience. I was totally caught up in friends, sports, cars, and newfound freedom. Although I sometimes observed Dad interacting in the community, I had no idea of the responsibility and danger his job could entail. As I entered my late teens and early 20s, people would share interesting stories about him. I learned more about some of the close calls that could have cost him his life, which he always downplayed in discussions with my mother and me.

As he was nearing his retirement at age 70, I asked Dad if he would take some time to record some of the more interesting and dramatic events of his career. I am so thankful that I did because he died of a massive heart attack only a few months after we made the tapes. My original plan was to just hold on to the tapes for the grandkids to hear at a later date. However, as I listened to them, I realized that there was a rich story that could be told by the right person.

Dr. Hal McAlister and I become close friends through our association at Georgia State University. After he retired, Hal expressed to me his interest in writing. I knew he was the right person to give the tapes to. Dr. McAlister has the gift of making a story come to life. I have experienced this first hand in watching him address a group of middle school students in the morning and a group of scientists in the afternoon all on the same subject while keeping them spellbound.

Dr. McAlister listened to the tapes and immediately was immersed in the Carlton Lewis story. As he began to share his notes, I knew we were going to convey a story that would shed a different light on Southern policing during a critical time in our state's history.

Chief Carlton Lewis was not perfect, but he did his best to serve all law-abiding citizens in his community regardless of race, gender, or socioeconomic standing. He would not be considered politically correct in today's society where law enforcement officers are constantly under attack for trying to do their job. Of course, there are some bad policemen, but most officers put on their uniforms every day before they put their lives at risk to protect and serve the public.

Chief Lewis once said "To be a good policeman, you have got to love people and you have got to want to help people. If you see a person take advantage of somebody, it makes you mad and it makes you want to take up for them. You want to take his place. You have to punish the guilty to take care of the innocent."

This Book is dedicated to the thousands of police officers across our country who are just like my dad. They all deserve the credit and recognition.

— Thomas Carlton Lewis
Senior Vice President for External Affairs,
Georgia State University, 1991-2009
Chief of Staff for
Governor Joe Frank Harris, 1985-1991
Cartersville, Georgia

Introduction

This book is an unlikely collaboration between a governmental affairs expert – Tom Lewis – who served as chief of staff to former Georgia Governor Joe Frank Harris and a retired professor of astronomy – me. We became colleagues and friends years ago through joint efforts to fund an astronomical research facility at Georgia State University. That adventure was a long and successful one but irrelevant to this book.

Tom was born and reared in Greene County, Georgia, an hour or so east of Atlanta. When he was a teenager, his father, at age 48, took a sharp turn in life by switching from a successful career in retail sales to policing. Many would see this as a rash act of a mid-life crisis that would be the ruination of a comfortable family. For Carlton Lewis, it was a reach for his destiny.

This is the story of what fate dealt him over the ensuing 22 years. We often remark that someone was born too early or too late for their times. In Carlton's case, the timing was nearly perfect. When he put on a badge in 1964, the South was about to emerge – kicking and screaming in many cases – from racial discrimination older than the Nation itself. Carlton was a son of the deep South whose grandfather had been a slave owner. His home was in a "50-50" county with nearly equal numbers of blacks and whites. Would Carlton Lewis, as an officer of the law, use his police powers to treat all the citizens of Greene County equally and fairly? Would he have a sympathetic and compassionate view of Greene's African Americans or would he, as happened elsewhere, employ dogs and firehoses on them? It was this question that most intrigued me about putting Carlton's story into written words.

What was Carlton Lewis thinking when he took this abrupt swerve toward a new future? How would he conduct himself as a lawman? What impact would he have on his community? Was he another Bull Conner in the making? Carlton would be a policeman for 22 years during which his actions would speak for themselves.

Answers to these questions were sought from contemporary newspaper articles, interviews with still-living Greene County residents who knew him, and recollections from his son Tom. Especially valuable is a taped interview of Carlton that Tom made in early 1986. More than a glimmer of his character and his suitability to his profession comes from comments Carlton made at the beginning of that interview and reiterated by his actions throughout his career.

Reading a transcript of Carlton's words relieves some concern that this man would become a head-knocker – a bully of a policeman who had no business with a badge and gun. Hearing his own voice from the taped interview gives one even more confidence that Carlton Lewis was likely an exceptionally empathetic cop.

Policing was remarkably different then from now. While Carlton was extremely well suited to his rough and tumble world of law enforcement two generations ago, he would not be cut out as a policeman today. Nor could most contemporary officers have made it in Carlton's world where rules and procedures factored little, and, buddy, you were on your own.

Carlton served for nine years as a deputy and then senior deputy to the legendary Sheriff L. L. Wyatt and then another 13 years as Chief of Police of Union Point, Greene's second largest city. Both departments had a meager two to four uniformed officers. Today, the Sheriff's Office is ten times larger but serves a population only half again the size it was in the 70s. A situation for which a SWAT team would today be called in would have been handled by a single officer in Carlton's day, often leading him into hair-raising encounters that provide a flow of stories to enlighten and entertain.

Most of these vignettes come from the 1986 recording. Tom's wisdom in having his father verbally memorialize the highlights of his career is a lesson to us all. Additional stories come from recent interviews of key individuals who knew Carlton. The majority of the dialogue herein is taken from those interviews with varying degrees of imagination thrown in for continuity and story-telling purposes. This is thus a mostly non-fiction book albeit one that is inevitably tilted toward the perspective of those who gave us their recollections. In some cases, those stories are best told in Carlton's own words from 1986, while in others they are well suited to an overlay of re-enactment dialogue consistent with his recorded words. I've used real names except in a few cases to protect privacy. However, there is one purely fictional character, a friend I invented for Carlton – Judge Ellis Buchanan – with whom situations and outcomes could be explained in dialogue, much of which was taken verbatim from the 1986 audio interview.

Tom and I acknowledge with our sincerest gratitude the folks who truly enabled this book through their personal experiences with Tom's father and their gracious hospitality in conveying their recollections to us. Carey Williams, Editor of *The Herald-Journal*, whose knowledge of that corner of the state, its people, and politics is justifiably legendary, gave us a wonderful morning at his newspaper headquarters on Main Street in Greensboro. After that session with Carey, I knew for sure there was a book in this. We met Johnny Grimes for a memorable lunch at the Cracker Barrel in Conyers, Georgia. Johnny, a retired Lt. Colonel of the Georgia State Patrol, transitioned from the one-man show of Carlton's time to modern law enforcement to attain the second tier of top command of our state police. His memories of the rip-roaring aspects of policing with

Carlton brought those days alive. Wayne Jackson was the Union Point City Clerk in Carlton's time and had a front-row seat on what transpired in his hometown, which included several of the most dramatic episodes we recount. Jill Rhodes and her husband Lanier, Union Point's present mayor, own the Rhodes Sports Corner and General Store, a must-see when you visit Union Point. Jill told us what Carlton meant to her children providing a complementary view to Carlton the tough cop, and Lanier expanded upon the reassuring presence Carlton projected in their community. Greensboro florist and Greene County Historian Joel McCray related a memory of Carlton's heart-warming resolution of a Peacock problem he had as a boy. Mary and Harold Finch were friends of the Lewises and went on many First Baptist Church outings with them over the years commencing before Carlton became a policeman. All of these kind people breathed life into this book.

I'm grateful to my good friend Tom for entrusting his father's stories to me. This book was enabled by his action more than three decades ago to sit his father down with a tape recorder. Of course, Tom read the book at each major revision to keep me in the right lane on this trip through Carlton's life. Patty Lewis likewise provided fine advice along the way.

I am especially honored that Governor Joe Frank Harris so kindly read the manuscript and contributed the book's foreword.

My law-professor daughter Merritt read an early draft of the book and critiqued the discussions of the appellate process following the convictions resulting from the Reuben Flynt murder. Merritt and my wife Susan both made the book more readable through their many suggestions. Judge Buchanan resulted from Merritt's thoughts on the book's first draft. I thank Susan whose patience and support remain key to all I do in this forty-sixth year of our marriage just as it was in our first.

I never met Carlton Lewis, but through working on this book with his son, I feel that I've gotten to know him pretty well. I wish I could have gone coon hunting with Carlton and Tom out there in the woods of Greene County and listened through the night to Carlton's recollections, told to the music of his coon-chasing dogs barking off in the darkness.

— Hal McAlister
Decatur, Georgia

Prologue

From The Herald-Journal
Greensboro, Georgia
Friday, October 31, 1969

BIG RATTLER KILLED

A big rattler indeed — now retired from the snake business. Just a typical day for a policeman in a rural Georgia "Mayberry?"

Maybe.

Maybe not.

Chap 1 — The Quiet House of Reuben Flynt

Union Point, Georgia
Monday, December 15, 1975, about 1:30 pm

Drawing his .38 Smith and Wesson, Carlton took a deep breath and slowly opened the front door. With all senses alert to a possible partner of the man he'd already arrested and jailed, his entry was met by utter silence — the stillness of an empty house. He'd sent an officer racing out North Rhodes Street to where it intersected the Washington Highway with strict orders to await his arrival. That officer was now ten paces behind him, a shotgun at port arms. Carlton Lewis glanced back at the man, caught his eye, and with a downward point of his finger indicated that he stand guard at the entry and go no farther.

Expecting the worst from the blood he'd seen on the wallet, Carlton advanced across the living room to the heart of the house. It had been around noon that Reuben had gone home from the bank for lunch, so Carlton headed for the kitchen. The room was in shambles — obviously the result of a violent fight. And, there, beside the kitchen table with its uneaten sandwich and spilt bottle of Coca Cola, he found worse than the worst.

Reuben Flynt lay sprawled on the floor, as still as the rest of the house. A thickening and darkening pool of blood haloed his head. Carlton had seen a lot in his nine years as a Deputy Sheriff of Greene County, Georgia, and more recently as Union Point Chief of Police — things he would not relate in any detail to his wife Eleanor. Those past acts of inhumanity paled in comparison with the violence that had befallen Reuben. His face was a pulverized facsimile of the bank vice president long held in the highest regard by his customers and community. Holstering his revolver, Carlton slowly shook his head. How in God's good world could such cruelty be visited upon this kind man?

The extent of that cruelty, apparently the result of a relentless beating with some sort of bludgeon, would deepen when Carlton knelt as close as he could without stepping into the blood or touching the body. The air went out of his lungs as he saw three or maybe four gunshot entry points into Reuben's face. They had been obscured by the mutilation from the clubbing, but there they were. Shot point blank in the face several times and then clubbed? Or was he clubbed and then shot?

Either way, murder in the commission of a bank robbery is a federal offense. It was time to call in the FBI and the GBI, the highly esteemed Georgia Bureau of Investigation. Without looking back and as if lowering the lid of a coffin, Carlton slowly closed the kitchen door. He quietly briefed the officer at the entry on the situation, ordering him to continue his watch and let no one enter. Ignoring representatives from the press now arriving on the scene, he proceeded to his car to radio for assistance from the Greene County Sheriff's Office in locking down the crime scene. The cruiser's flashers and siren would get him to his office in under three minutes. He would call in the feds and the GBI before making the eight-mile drive at high speed to Greensboro where Reuben's wife taught at the high school. There, with a few brief words, Chief Lewis would forever darken the skies of Mrs. Flynt's world.

Union Point, Georgia
Monday, December 15, 1975, an hour earlier

Union Point, about an hour and a half east of Atlanta out I-20, had a population of around 1,700 in 1975. Tracing its origins back to the early 1800s, the little settlement eventually got its name as a result of the Atlanta, Augusta, and Athens railroads converging there before going on their separate ways. Life was good in Union Point, and the nearly 20 million pairs of socks produced each year by the Union Manufacturing knitting mill gave steady work to several hundred of its citizens. A long block on Sibley Avenue, just around the corner from City Hall, which also housed the town's three-man police department, provided stores where folks could spend some of that money earned in their shifts at the mill.

Strolling that block along Sibley takes you past Rhodes Drug Store, Morgan Furniture, a provider of hardware and clothing, a second pharmacy, an auto parts store, and Dr. Billy Rhodes' medical office. Cross Fluker Street at the end of the block, and you arrive at the entrance to The Farmers Bank, "proudly serving Union Point since 1911."

Just before 1:00 pm, Derwin Young paused at the bank's front door and glanced across Sibley where his Uncle Charlie stood about 250 feet away on the downslope from the old and now defunct Terrace Inn Hotel on the other side of the railroad tracks. Charlie was presumably standing watch in the plan he'd hatched at Reuben Flynt's just minutes ago. Derwin wondered just what Charlie could do other than head for the hills, taking their getaway car with him, if the police showed up. But there was no turning back now. He patted Reuben's wallet stuffed in his right front pocket and pulled open the bank's door. An unoccupied teller stood at her window nearest the entrance.

Taking the wallet from his pocket and laying it on the counter, Derwin told the teller, "The man that give me this billfold said for you to give me $60,000 or he will kill Reuben Flynt in fifteen minutes." She stared at him before turning away to take Derwin's instructions to the bank's president, Ben Stewart. All of this was witnessed by JoAnn Cathie who was in a back office at the bank. She called City Hall where Union Point City Clerk Wayne Jackson wore many hats, one of which was that of occasional police dispatcher.

JoAnn whispered over the phone that somebody was robbing the bank.

Carlton was on a routine patrol when his radio crackled. He glanced at his watch noting the time as 12:49. Wayne's calm voice came out of the low-fidelity speaker giving little hint that something serious was at hand.

"Carlton, this is Wayne," who then paused before continuing. "Carlton, go by the bank" – another pause – "I, uh, think they're robbin' it now." This news was conveyed in the same tone of urgency Wayne might use in reporting a cat stuck up a tree over on Newsome Street, but it was clear and effective in getting the Chief's attention.

Carlton wheeled his car around, flipped on the flashers but not the siren, and headed for the bank. He pulled in beside the building, grabbing his 12-gauge as he got out of the car.

Shotgun in hand, Carlton walked to the corner of the building and glanced up and down Sibley. All was normal.

Had he looked over across the tracks, he would have seen an astonished man trotting towards a car. At the sight of a cop with a shotgun, Charlie was doing exactly what his nephew thought he'd do – vamoosing.

The owner of the café just down the other way ran up to Carlton.

"What's up, Chief," he asked wide eyed.

"Somebody's robbin' the bank, Willis. You need to get back in your place away from here!" And Willis did just that.

A lady came out of the bank, saw Carlton, and hurried up to him.

"Mr. Carlton, they got the Vice President back in the vault," she told him. He would shortly find out this information was inaccurate.

Carlton worried they might hurt Reuben and was about to run into the bank when another lady approached to conduct her business inside. With no apparent concern over a police officer with a shotgun standing beside the door and lights flashing on his cruiser, she was indignant when Carlton told her "Ma'am, you got to get out of here right now!" He had to shoo away several other customers wanting to do some banking over the lunch hour.

At this point, people were coming out of nearby stores and offices to see what was going on. Even a train stopped early so the crew could watch. Carlton remembered the building had no back door. The robbers had to come out the front. Plan changed – he would stay outside to divert customers while waiting for the robber or robbers to leave. He positioned himself away from the front window to stay out of sight and at an angle so when he fired the sawed-off any buckshot missing his man would impact the building and not the gawkers in the growing crowd.

Then, a quick glance through the window showed a man heading to the door, a big paper sack in one hand, Ben Stewart in the other. Apparently seeing Carlton, the bank officer jerked away and ran backwards from the robber just as the man stepped outside.

Carlton yelled, "Freeze, or I'll kill ya!"

The sack hit the pavement, and two hands launched high in the air. End of robbery. Carlton approached but kept enough distance so the man couldn't lunge for the shotgun. He got out his revolver and cocked it while ordering the man to put both hands against the block wall of the bank and spread his feet. He pressed the pistol's barrel against the man's skull.

"You make a move and I'll blow your brains out!"

No move would be made.

Carlton waved for a man in the crowd to come over. Pistol still against the robber's head, Carlton handed the shotgun to the civilian telling him to keep it on his prisoner so he could cuff him.

Seeing the situation under control, Ben Stewart came outside. "Carlton, bring him back in here. I got to tell you something."

So, Carlton retrieved his shotgun and escorted his prisoner to the banker's office where he learned of the $60,000 demand, was given Reuben Flynt's bloody wallet, and told that their vice president had not returned to the office after taking his lunch at home.

Ten minutes later, with his prisoner locked up in a departmental cell behind City Hall, Union Point Police Chief Carlton Lewis was rocketing toward Reuben's home, lights flashing and siren screaming.

Union Point, late 1975

When Carlton finally returned to Union Point after discovering Reuben Flynt's body, he and others immediately began questioning Derwin Young, who gave up his uncle right off the bat. It turned out that Charlie's grandmother lived in Greensboro, which precipitated another high-speed trip back to the county seat after alerting Sheriff Wyatt of the likelihood that a murderer was holed up there. Charlie was promptly arrested and equally promptly confessed. Both perpetrators were subsequently transferred to neighboring Clarke County where they were incarcerated in that county's jail in Athens. Home to the University of Georgia, Athens had a larger and more secure lockup. It also took the prisoners away from the community whose soul they had terribly wounded.

Reuben Flynt had been very highly regarded by members of both the white and black communities. Concern arose that outraged citizens, especially from among the black residents who Reuben had helped with any number of banking transactions over the years, might want to get at these murderers. This was surprising to some because Reuben was white while Charlie and Derwin were black.

On the front page of its December 19, 1975 issue, *The Herald-Journal*, Greensboro's and Greene County's primary newspaper, described the scene prior to the transfer to Athens as well as the effect Reuben's brutal death had on the people of Union Point. For the next few days, the paper reiterated the high regard held by all who knew him.

"'He was one of the finest men you'd want to know,' said his pastor, Rev. Emory Cartrett of the First Methodist Church in Union Point, 'He was the treasurer of our church.'"

"'It was a shame for a man's life to be wiped out like that,' neighbors were saying after the extortion attempt at Farmers Bank had ended in Flynt's murder. 'He was such a nice man...a Christian worker. If I had to say who was the nicest man in Greene County I'd say Reuben Flynt...'"

"'He beat him unmercifully and killed him,' said a local news person who had been with officers when the body was found."

"The tragedy of the event surfaced when law officials rushed to Flynt's home and found his body. 'You read about things like this happening in Detroit or Atlanta, but you just don't think of it happening here,' residents where saying to each other."

"Flynt himself, neighbors said, had been a model citizen. He was active in church and civic affairs but stayed out of the limelight. 'He was well respected and well liked,' area residents said. 'He was the kind of person you could just tell you needed something, and he'd tell you to write a check for it and come by the bank and make a note on it...' Flynt, they said, was also a real gentleman. 'He was always dressed in a coat and tie, and you know, people around here just don't usually dress like that.'"

"Neighbors were shocked and saddened, even frightened. 'I hope they got them all,' one resident remarked outside of city hall. 'I want to be able to sleep tonight.'"

"'We got both defendants,' Sheriff Wyatt told news people Monday night at the Greene County Courthouse. 'Of course, we can't say yet whether they have confessed, but one will be charged with murder, and the other possibly with accessory...'"

Derwin and Charlie Young were given speedy trials in Greene County Superior Court. Both were convicted of armed robbery and robbery by intimidation for which they got life in prison on the first charge and 20 years for the second. Additionally, Charlie had been charged with malice murder for which he was sentenced to death.

✝ ✝ ✝

"Good mornin', Miz Huff," Ellis greeted as he entered Huff's Diner and headed for his usual booth farthest from the door. "I forget, is this the month when you change the grease in that deep fryer of yours?" he continued without looking back.

"No, Judge, that won't be 'til the fall," she replied, "but I'll add a tablespoon of fresh lard before dropping in your catfish today. I wouldn't do that for nobody else."

He paused and turned to her. "That's mighty kind of you, Beatrice, to worry about my nutrition like you do." He continued on and slid into "his" booth to wait for Carlton.

Ellis Buchanan was known to all Greene Countians. He had been their Magistrate Court judge for nearly 15 years before being elected to represent them in the state legislature for another 20. At that juncture, he retired from politics and stayed home to full-time private practice for another decade. He got his start in law when he graduated number one in his class from the University of Georgia law school in 1919 at the tender age of 20. By age 25, he was a partner in the Atlanta Law firm of King & Spalding.

But, that trajectory did not satisfy Ellis Buchanan, and he decided to jump off the big-money legal career train and head back home to Greene County to work for the people he knew best. Not wishing to live in the bustle of the "big city" of Greensboro, Ellis settled in Union Point, married a local girl, and raised a family in a house across the railroad tracks from the Sibley Avenue row of business. Nearby was Beatrice Huff's diner, which he frequented for lunch virtually every day since he abruptly retired following his wife's passing. It was at "Miz Huff's" where he crossed paths with Carlton Lewis even before Carlton entered policing and their unlikely friendship commenced.

Looking out the window spanning Huff's street-side row of

booths, Ellis scanned up and down Lamb Avenue, but there was no Carlton in sight. Then, to his surprise, Carlton walked out from the kitchen. Ellis started to ask, "why the heck...," but he stopped short when he saw deep concern on Carlton's face and a folded newspaper held tight in his left hand. Carlton laid it on the table so Ellis could see the short article. The Judge held up Carlton's wrinkled copy of *The Atlanta Constitution*, and his expression abruptly switched to resemble his friend's after reading only the brief headline, "Court Overturns Conviction in Slaying." He didn't need to read further as he had anticipated this outcome when the Eleventh Circuit agreed to hear arguments on appeal by Charlie Young's new attorney. But, the ruling floored Carlton, who could not understand how such a thing could happen.

Beatrice Huff walked up with two cups of coffee and was about to let loose with a clever reply to Ellis concerning restaurant deep fat fryers. But, when she saw the downcast looks of her two most regular customers, she sat the cups down and departed without a word.

"Can you believe it?!" Carlton's tone was a mix of anger and astonishment. "You think they'll let that murdering SOB go? He's guilty as sin, and they throw out his conviction?!"

Ellis held up both palms towards Carlton.

"Now, hold your horses there, Carlton. I told you during the trial that old Garland was giving him incompetent defense."

"Yeah, I got that, but, dammit, he confessed."

"Dudn't matter. The constitution guarantees your right to competent legal representation during trial. It doesn't have to be perfect, but Reuben Garland had been practicing law for sixty years and shouldn't have taken this on in the first place at his age. He was one of the greats in his heyday, but you can't maintain that edge forever. I'm living proof of that."

After a short pause, Ellis continued, "You might keep that in mind for yourself, Chief."

Carlton glared at him. "I ain't eighty years old quite yet, Your

Honor."

Ellis nodded and turned his attention to stirring two sugars into his coffee. Carlton took a sip from his own cup – no cream, no sugar.

Ellis took a shot at guessing why the three-judge federal appeals court panel ruled as it did.

"I haven't read the panel's decision, but I'd bet my bar license that it first points to Garland's attempt at an insanity plea when he had no prior evidence to support it and kept at it even after the state presented testimony to the contrary."

"So, he wasn't crazy. Doesn't mean you throw out the conviction," Carlton objected.

Ellis sighed, "First off, the appellate panel didn't 'throw out' the conviction, they denied the appeal to a *habeas* writ from the lower federal district court and ordered it carried out. Charlie Young will be retried, and this time by a competent attorney who won't go chasing that insanity rabbit down a hole. That approach amounted to no defense at all."

Carlton just stared at him while Ellis lifted up his cup and downed the whole thing as if it were a shot of Jack Daniels.

"How do you do that, Ellis?"

Ignoring the question, Ellis put down the empty cup and continued debriefing the Charlie Young situation to his friend.

"But, there's more. You can only be executed in this state for murdering somebody if it's premeditated or done in the commission of an armed robbery. If someone kills you in the heat of passion, your family may want him fried in the electric chair, but the law says he's committed voluntary manslaughter and goes to jail for life, not to death row."

"And, then he gets paroled even from that someday, don't he?" asked Carlton.

"Yep. That's also a possibility under the law and is probably what Young will get at some point down the line."

"But, what about Reuben's wallet? Young took that from him and he had a gun. That's armed robbery in my book!"

"Could be, but the more probable scenario – one that a good attorney could get a jury to buy – is that Young got upset when Reuben told him to go back to the office and wait on him rather than addressing his concern about the two delinquent notes his grandmother had co-signed with him. He didn't want Reuben going after granny, and he wanted Reuben's assurance to that right away, not in half an hour after Reuben leisurely ate his sandwich. Push led to shove, Reuben was killed, and the wallet thing was an incredibly dumb afterthought."

Carlton understood all this, but it did not make him feel much better.

"You know, Ellis, I feel like so much that I do is for nuthin'. I catch somebody who's done something awful and deserves a cell door welded shut on him. Then he goes into the judicial system and gets off easy or even let go! Even if it involves such a terrible thing as what Young did to Reuben. I just can't accept that."

Ellis picked up his cup for a thoughtful sip before remembering he had already emptied it. He lowered it back on the table.

"As the Chief of Police of Union Point, you played the major role in solving this crime swiftly and bringing Charlie and Derwin Young to justice. How do you think things would have gone had Wyatt been waiting at the bank door instead of you?"

Carlton smiled at that question.

"Why, the Sheriff would 'a cut Derwin in half with that shotgun."

"You're darn right he would have, and, who knows, Charlie might have evaded capture, since Derwin wouldn't be there to give him up in a heartbeat."

Carlton looked skeptical.

"My point is, Carlton, that you did a courageous and outstanding job terminating that crime during its commission thereby allowing the arrest of all guilty parties. You handed those boys over to the prosecution and the courts on a silver platter. You were done at that point."

"You think so?" Carlton asked.

"I know so. I also know that what has today happened in the courts was the right thing, the only outcome consistent with our Constitution."

As Beatrice walked back over to their table to see if they were ready to order, Carlton had one last question.

"How soon might Young be paroled?"

Ellis grinned at him, "I wouldn't concern myself about that, Carlton. You and I will probably both be dead and gone well before then."

Hearing that last sentence, Beatrice took up the thread.

"And I might be dead before you boys get around to ordering. How about it. Want your usuals?"[1]

Chap 2 — The Path to Policing

County Greene was carved out of Washington County by the Georgia General Assembly on February 3, 1786. Named for Revolutionary War General Nathanael Greene, the new county was near the state's western frontier beyond which was still, but not for much longer, the domain of the Creek Indians who had ceded the land to the young state only three years earlier. That Georgia's capital would one day be located some 70 miles west of Greene County in a place called Atlanta, home to nearly 6 million, was beyond anyone's wildest imaginings.

Greene is located in the middle of the Piedmont region, known for its "Georgia red clay" and a climate ideal for crops like soybeans, wheat, and, especially, cotton. Summer highs typically max out at a bit over 100 and winters rarely go south of 20. This makes for short, bleak winters and long, steamy summers with cicadas rattling the daytime and crickets punctuating the night. Those summers yield a lengthy growing season for cotton with its massive labor requirements for cultivation and harvest.

Greene County had 5,405 inhabitants at the time of the first U.S. census in 1790; a number that more than doubled by 1810. From the beginning, cotton dominated the county's economy while demanding a large labor force so that by 1860 nearly 45% of the state's population was comprised of enslaved Africans. In that census, though, Greene County had twice as many black slaves as free white citizens. Today, Greene is a "50-50 county." The county's population peaked in 1920 at 20,306 souls. At that time, a large hosiery mill at Union Point had become the major employer, but the boll weevil demolished cotton farming by the 1920s and the Great Depression was around the corner. By 1960, the population had dwindled to 11,193 – nearly 500 fewer than in 1810.

✛ ✛ ✛ ✛

Carlton Lewis was born on March 31, 1916 in Sparta,[2] Georgia, the seat of Greene's neighboring county of Hancock. His parents were Thomas Jefferson Lewis (1878-1930) and Pearl Darden Lewis (1888-1928).[3] Family lore had it that the family descended from *the* Thomas Jefferson. Veneration of the Founding Fathers also shows in the naming of Carlton's great-grandfather, James Madison Lewis, who came from Virginia to Georgia where he died in 1843.

It turns out there is a family connection to President Jefferson in the person of Meriwether Lewis, Jefferson's personal secretary sent west in 1803 with William Clark to search for a viable route to the Pacific. Meriwether Lewis was born in 1774 in Albemarle County, Virginia, home to Jefferson's exquisite Monticello as well as his University of Virginia in Charlottesville.

Carlton's grandfather William Jefferson Lewis was born 1836 in Georgia. William married Mary J. Stewart in 1859.[4] On May 5, 1862, William enlisted in the Georgia 55th Infantry Regiment as a private in Company B, formed from Greene County men and known as Stocks Volunteers.[5] Unlike most Confederate infantry who were poor farmers with no property, real or human, William went away to war as the holder of four slaves.[6]

He was released from service in June 1863 as the result of chronic rheumatism, an obsolete term for arthritis, which if severe enough could render a man incapable of military service.[7] Had he not been discharged early, likely as not William would have joined with most of the others of his regiment who were captured at the Battle of the Cumberland Gap on September 9, 1863.

Instead, William returned home to Hancock County and settled back into farming there for the rest of his life, undoubtedly suffering regularly from his "rheumatism." He died in 1911 – "worn out from work" as his great-grandson Tom would later recall – so Carlton never knew him, but his grandmother Mary survived until 1925.[8]

Carlton's father, Thomas J. Lewis, was the next-to-last of William's and Mary's seven children. Thomas and Pearl Lewis had nine children, seven of whom were girls: Morris, Viola, Inez, Willie Mae, Carlton, Edna, Agnes, Edith, and Clarice. Sometime between the 1920 and 1930 censuses, Thomas relocated from Hancock to Greene, settling in Union Point, where he, Inez, and Willie Mae worked at the hosiery mill. Pearl had died in 1928, and Thomas passed away two years later.

Carlton thus lost his mother at age 12 and his father at 14. His brother Morris had a wife of his own by 1930 and would shortly relocate to North Carolina where he would live out his life. Carlton, although still a boy, was the oldest male at home when his father died, and he went to live with his uncle Charles E. Lewis. His siblings were sent off to the care of other relatives. By 1940, Carlton was 24 and the head of a household in Union Point living with his sisters Willie Mae, Agnes, and Edith. He was a knitter while Willie Mae and Agnes were loopers at the hosiery mill. Edith was still in school.

This arrangement was interrupted by Pearl Harbor, and, like so many young American men, Carlton enlisted. He entered the Navy on April 15, 1942 for the duration of the war and was released from the service four days before Christmas, 1945.[9]

Following basic training, Carlton was assigned to an auxiliary aircraft carrier with a crew of 860 officers and men. After arriving for service at Pearl Harbor in early November 1943, the vessel soon steamed for the Gilbert Islands to launch strikes on Makin Island during the Thanksgiving season and to support invasion forces there. She returned to San Diego to pick up new aircraft and then returned to Hawaii over Christmas to prepare for the Battle of Kwajalein. Originally christened the *Coral Sea*, Carlton's ship was renamed the *Anzio* in September 1944.[10]

Carlton often told his friends and family how his ship's captain allowed the men to blow off steam built up between them in the ship's close quarters by letting them resolve their differences in boxing matches. In one such bout, a ship-mate with a reputation of a bruiser was challenging people to fight him – anyone would do just fine. Carlton looked around the carrier deck expecting a shipmate to rise to the challenge. Seeing there were no takers, he shrugged, stepped forward and said he was game for it. The men cheered, and bets were quickly placed with all of Carlton's buddies putting their money on him. Carlton strapped on gloves and climbed through the ropes into the ring. Somebody clanged a bell. His opponent launched his attack, clobbering him. Carlton never landed a blow and was soon horizontal on the deck. He lost his buddies' gambling money, but he gained their respect as someone always up for a fight, no matter the odds.

Carlton Lewis aboard the Anzio

In September 1945, Carlton wrote a letter home to his sister Viola describing the wartime service he'd seen. At the end of that letter, he told her, "Considering all the above, you can see why I'm proud to be aboard the *Anzio*. While this isn't an official Navy release, I can vouch for the truth of every statement, and it's perfectly okay if you want to let our home town paper print any of it. Your Brother, Carlton Lewis." Viola sent it to *The Herald-Journal*, and it was printed in its entirety.

In the letter, Carlton reported that since commissioned in August 1943, his ship had "covered 160,000 miles of the blue Pacific, launching fighters and torpedo bombers for a total of 7,000 sorties, and that ain't bad." He listed the *Anzio's* battle stations: the Gilberts, Kwajalein, Emirau Island, Saipan, Tinian, and Guam. The Big A, as her crew called her, was in the Philippine Sea in December 1944, when a typhoon with 110 mph winds sank three destroyers around her, the *Anzio* rolling heavily in the high seas but staying afloat. She then went on to Iwo Jima where Carlton witnessed the sinking of the *Bismarck Sea* on February 21, 1945 following two kamikaze hits, taking 318 souls down with her. At war's end, the *Anzio* was busy hunting subs a couple of hundred miles off the coast of Japan.

Carlton was proud of his service. Whenever the War came up in conversation, he would speak of learning to fight through military training that was ingrained in him for the rest of his life. Carlton recognized that he had relished fighting since he was a boy while most of his friends avoided it if at all possible. As he matured, he understood that enjoying a good fight was just part of who he was. Why bother to try to understand it? In later years, he was grateful for this predilection as it sure had served him well when he wound up being a policeman.

Following his discharge, Carlton returned to Georgia and went into two or three different kinds of business, none of which completely satisfied hm. He was trained to fight, had done so during the war, and fighting grew to be a key component of his determination to find a career that he truly enjoyed.

In the meantime, Carlton's business attempts included tire recapping followed by partnering in a dry-cleaning business that expanded to a three-county operation before he sold it in 1952. He next bought a Sinclair station in Union Point where he pumped gas for 24¢ a gallon in the late 1950s. After a few years of selling fuel, repairing tires, changing oil, and doing minor auto repair work, Carlton switched gears again and went to work for the Standard Coffee Company selling their products directly to residents along his multi-county route. He must have been quite a salesman as he grew his business to become Standard's top salesman in Georgia. It wasn't that these ways of earning a living weren't working out; they were and would provide a good means for raising a family. He yearned for something consistent with his nature.

And then, in 1964, his search for a good fight was fulfilled. Carlton was approached about becoming a deputy to Greene County Sheriff Loy Lee Wyatt. "L. L." Wyatt, as he was invariably referred to, had first won the office of Sheriff in 1940 and every election since then. L. L. would stand at the top of the ranks nationally of those who had held these offices as a result of his longevity, bravery, and audacity in serving the people of his County for 52 years. This was the remarkable man under whom Carlton embarked on his new career in policing.

L. L. was one of those larger than life characters whose lawman exploits would eventually attract a Hollywood producer and screenwriter. A Greene County historic marker outside Greenesboro's historic jail nicely summarizes his story:

SHERIFF L. L. WYATT

This 1895 jail is named for the legendary Sheriff, Loy Lee Wyatt, who enforced the laws in Greene County for fifty-two years until his death in 1977. Sheriff L. L. Wyatt was born on January 2, 1904, in Paulding County. He was recruited to serve the citizens of Greene County due to his fast legs and honest reputation. In 1925, L. L. Wyatt began his law enforcement career as a Greene County policeman who waged a "one-man war" against the making of illegal corn whiskey. Prior to his arrival, moonshine production was considered the leading industry in Greene County and its produce was enjoyed in all of the finest hotels of Atlanta. After having rid the County of its moonshiners, Wyatt ran for the Office of Sheriff in 1940 defeating the incumbent. He served as Sheriff until he died in 1977. At the time of his death he was the longest standing Sheriff in the State.

During his 37 years as Sheriff, Wyatt became a legend in his own time. He was a religious man who believed that God blessed him with protection during all of his fights, gun battles, and dangerous encounters. His law enforcement exploits exposed him to at least five gunshot wounds in the line of duty, in part due to the fact that he seldom carried a gun on his person, requiring him to retrieve it from his car at the sight of danger. In the early days of his career, when moonshiners resisted arrest, Wyatt regularly shot it out with them. He killed over a half dozen men, all of whom shot at him first.

The most famous gunfight of Sheriff Wyatt´s career occurred in 1974. He was 70 years old at the time. Bank robbers eluded a 100-car police chase that started in Wrens, Georgia, and ended in Greene County. The bank robbers had killed a teller at the bank in Wrens and had taken two women hostages. Sheriff Wyatt set up a road block midway between Union Point and Greensboro. Wyatt stood in the middle of the road as the speeding car approached. The robbers attempted to shoot him, but the gun misfired. One bank robber was killed in the ensuing battle, but both women were unharmed. Sheriff Wyatt subsequently received the award of the Peace Officer of the Year for his bravery in this incident.

Sheriff Wyatt was a family man, devoted to his wife, son, and grandchildren. He was a businessman, lending his experience to the operation and affairs of the Citizens Union Bank as a director. He was a community leader who had concern for all citizens — rich and poor, black and white. Out of a concern for these people, legend has it that Sheriff Wyatt confronted a notorious member of the Dixie Mafia and proclaimed, "These are my people and I want you to leave them alone!"

Sheriff Wyatt, also known as Mr. Sheriff, was the epitome of a community-oriented police officer long before such an idea was born and served as an example for every officer to follow.

Wyatt was 60 when Carlton hired on and had no intention of ever retiring. As a result of his age and experience, Carlton would become Wyatt's chief deputy and, by 1972, he was *de facto* Sheriff as a result of L. L.'s increasing age and focus on being the real power in Greene County's politics. The two had high mutual respect, which continued even after Carlton left the Sheriff's office in early 1974 to become Police Chief in Union Point. While there were important differences between the two men, we will see that Carlton's bravery and audacity were no less than that of his mentor L. L. Wyatt.[11]

Policing in 1964, as it always has, required dealing with the usual human misbehaviors, mayhem, and criminal acts to protect lives and property. On top of that, and even though Prohibition was history by the time Carlton pinned on a badge, moonshining was still a booming underground enterprise in Greene where the low population density and good access to Atlanta led enterprising cookers of corn to construct large stills along clear-running creeks to quench city dwellers' thirsty for untaxed ethanol. Busting up those backwoods distilleries was a continuing law-enforcement activity.

Like the majority of rural jurisdictions, each department consisted of only a handful of uniformed men. It was typical for only a single deputy sheriff to be on duty in an entire county at any one time. Cops had to be self-reliant as backups could be few and far between. Hand-to-hand combat with drunks and crazies was always just around the corner. Stating the obvious – policing was a dangerous business, then as now.

It could also be dangerous to those who got policed. Billy clubs could be whipped out in an instant to calm the unruly arrestee or to administer on-the-spot summary punishment. Hiring practices could be lax and training in rural communities was relatively superficial. Excessive force and outright brutality were pits that an officer might easily wander into – an outcome largely determined by one's character and empathy.

The summer prior to the 1964 election in which Johnson trounced Goldwater, LBJ convinced Congress to pass civil rights legislation dear to the heart of his assassinated predecessor. The Civil Rights Act of 1964 became the law of the land the very year Carlton Lewis became a deputy sheriff. This would have monumental repercussions on the "separate but equal" Jim Crow South.

Georgia's powerful Senator Richard B. Russell, Jr., born in Winder less than 50 miles northwest of Greene's county seat at Greensboro, led the Senate's Southern Bloc in opposing Johnson's Civil Rights bill. A staunch white supremacist, Russell had already directed successful efforts to defeat legislation that would have protected black citizens from lynching, ensured their right to vote, and provided them with equal treatment under the law. With the Democratic party's long-time hold on Georgia's U.S. Congress seats, Russell yet again ran unopposed in 1960 and 1966 and was re-elected with 99.95% of the votes to the office he had held since being appointed to it in 1933. He died in 1971 while still in office.

Into this stew of history, geography, demographics, and human nature, other ingredients were being stirred that would challenge Southern law enforcement for years to come. One reason for Johnson's runaway election was that he scared the nation out of its wits with dire exaggerations of Goldwater's warmongering tendencies. Greene went more than two-to-one for LBJ. Johnson then escalated the situation in Indochina into the terrible ground war that was Vietnam, in which Greene County was fortunate in only losing three men.[12]

On top of all this, the symbol for Southern law enforcement had been hammered into American culture since the mid-1950s in the person of T.E. "Bull" Conner, Birmingham's long-time public safety commissioner. During the 60s, at the peak of his notoriety, Conner promoted his segregationist agenda by refusing protection to Freedom Riders from thugs and Klansmen and unleashing dogs and fire hoses on demonstrators. By mid-decade, the race-relations pot was cranking up to full boil. When Carlton Lewis entered policing, the events at the Edmund Pettis Bridge were around the corner and the boil-over after the Lorraine Motel in Memphis just a few years away.[13]

This, then, was the environment Carlton Lewis catapulted into when, in 1964, he decided to undertake policing deep in a rural jurisdiction of the Old Confederacy populated at nearly 50% by the descendants of slaves. Northern "agitators" would invade his South and many long-revered political leaders were in lock step against integration in spite of new federal laws they had fought so long while tacitly, if not actively, encouraging head-knocking by the front-line cops.

What was Carlton Lewis thinking when he took this abrupt swerve toward a new future? How would he conduct himself as a lawman? What impact would he have on his community? Was he another Bull Conner in the making? Carlton would be a policeman for 22 years during which his actions would speak for themselves.

Chap 3 — Itching for a Fight

Carlton knew he was a born fighter. That's what eventually took him away from the civilian world of farming, dry cleaning, filling stations, and coffee services. He was bored with those common-place and unexciting activities and felt his life starting over as fate intended for him when he was hired as a Greene County deputy sheriff in 1964. He relished a good fight and never shied away out of fear or concern over getting walloped and hospitalized as happened more than once. At 5'11", he was not a big man, but he was stocky and well-muscled – a boxer's physique. His biggest disadvantage was his age. He was 45 when policing provided him opportunities as a fearless and natural fighter, and he continued to get into serious hand-to-hand combat with those needing some jail time until late into his fifties.

At the same time, he never killed or seriously injured anyone in his efforts to encourage them into the back seat of his patrol car. He knew when to call it quits as if some part of him was standing apart from the fight alert, arms folded and ready to whisper in his ear "all right, now, that's enough." It was that ability to not step over a line that prevented him from becoming a brutal policeman and perhaps even a criminal. He had a touch of humanity in him that we hope is in all officers of the law.

That said, if a good fight wouldn't come to him, he'd occasionally go looking for one.

During the Jim Crow era, Southern blacks could only find work in areas that either did not interest whites or required levels of physical exertion whites did not wish to expend. In Greene County, the logging and pulp wood industry was one such "profession" assigned to blacks. Try spending a stifling August week in the Georgia heat cutting brush, clearing, hauling, and manhandling timber toward its ultimate destination at a saw mill or turpentine plant and, regardless of your being black or white, you'd be ready to cut loose on Friday and Saturday nights. Of course, if you are black, you can't go into town and enjoy a few cold ones at a well-appointed drinking and eating establishment. You would need to find it outside the white man's province.

To fulfill that basic human need to recharge, so-called "juke joints" became commonplace throughout the South. Located well away from white communities, and often at rural crossroads to enhance their accessibility, juke joints were non-descript primitive structures wherein black men and women could find spirited drink, a limited food menu, and music. If so inclined, one could also do a bit of gambling or buy a jar of "Georgia moon" to take home. But, mostly, relaxation and fun after a back-busting week for very little money was the siren call of the weekend. Juke joints were something to look forward to while laboring in the 95°/95% heat and humidity of a typical summer day and a reset towards the return to those labors the following Monday. And, as a bonus, there were no whites at jukes.

Not surprisingly, things could sometimes get out of hand on these recuperative weekends. Too much alcohol and rambunctiousness could lead to fighting and even worse – knifings and shootings that would bring in the police. Also unsurprising was the eagerness not to be taken to jail for fighting on a Friday night thereby ruining the weekend. When confronted by the cops, that fervent desire could lead to a highly-motivated determination to resist arrest. On top of keeping the peace, Carlton took special interest in making sure juke joints respected the law of those days that, out of respect for Sunday's church activities, there could be no such irreverent recreation as too much drinking and dancing after midnights on Saturdays.

Johnny Grimes shared Carlton's fearlessness. He was the first black officer hired as a sheriff's deputy in Greene County and brought exceptional experience to the job after serving as an MP in the Air Force. He would later become only the fourth African American hired on the Georgia State Patrol wherein he rose to the rank of Lieutenant Colonel, the second highest command echelon of that organization.

Johnny recalls that during the time he rode with Carlton Lewis as a rookie officer, Carlton would occasionally announce at 2 am that it was time to go check on and maybe close up a juke joint or two. "Oh, boy," Johnny thought, "here we go again." So, off they'd go down some dirt road with the sounds of celebration gradually cranking up from the approaching establishment.

He characterized these late-night visits to juke joints as, at times, "having to fight your way in, and then fight your way out." He and Carlton would stride into a juke rollicking with music, dancing, and conversation all of which was kicked up a notch or two by the plentitude of booze on the premises. They would walk around looking for problems that might require their attention. Sometimes, their mere presence was adequate to the task of fulfilling the attention requirement. A word here followed by a word there and fists would be flying. Inevitably, the offending drunk would be handcuffed, tossed into the back of their car and locked in to await one or maybe two more men to haul off to the jail in Greensboro.

This would be so demoralizing to the remaining patrons as to effectively close down the place hours earlier than had been intended. Most of the time, Carlton would release those in his back seat after the crowd had dispersed feeling that he'd done a good night's work in shutting down the juke before any really harm got done that night. There was really no need to haul them off to jail after they had unwittingly cooperated to achieve his goal of an early closing for that particular joint. Time to call it a night and get some rest for the morning patrol and warrant distribution. Mission accomplished.

✢ ✢ ✢ ✢

"I thought I was going to need your services to fix a ticket for me today," Ellis told Carlton as they got settled into their booth at Miz Huff's, ready for a hot lunch on a cold February day.

Carlton grinned, "What for?" he asked.

"No, you shouldn't ask me 'what for,' you should ask me what cop stopped me?"

"Okay, Your Honor, I'll bite. Who stopped you?"

"Your old buddy Jimmy Kirk," Ellis answered and then clarified, "For a burnt-out break-light bulb, of all things."

"Ole Jimmy Kirk!" Carlton said louder than he should and slapped the table, rattling the utensils. Other diners glanced their way.

"I haven't seen that old boy in months. How's he doin'?"

Jimmy was a Georgia State Patrol officer stationed in Madison in next-door Morgan County. When the occasion arose, Carlton liked to work with Jimmy who didn't shy away from a good "tussle" when it was needed to gain control of a situation. At the same time, both didn't mind getting their fighting itch scratched when the opportunity arose.

"Seemed just fine. He was in a generous mood because he just gave me a warning about the tail light. He even tipped his Smokey-the-Bear hat at the end."

"That's 'cause he recognized you, Judge."

"Maybe so," Ellis acknowledged.

"Did I ever tell you about Jimmy and me goin' in that juke joint expecting an ambush?" asked Carlton.

"Yes, you did," Ellis replied, knowing he was destined to hear it again anyway.

"Jimmy was a fighter, just like I was. He loved to fight. And, he could fight, ole Jimmy could. I used to love to police with him. One day, I had been out at Daniel Springs where there was a dance goin' on at a juke joint I'd go out to on weekends because there was always a fight or two up there. So, I'd break it up and generally get one or two and take them out of there and lock 'em up."

"I see," Ellis courteously responded.

Carlton went on. "A couple of guys I'd put in jail told me they'd overheard some of the blacks talking in their cell. They said 'We'll get Carlton this weekend. Let him come out there. We'll be set for him.'"

"The state boys were holding a road check the next Saturday afternoon, and I went out there to join in. I was telling Jimmy about what was heard at the jail, and I said 'I got to know what they got in mind. I'm going out to that dance tonight, and I'm going to show them something. I am going to close that darn place down.'"

"So, Jimmy says, 'Can I go with you?'"

"I said, 'Yeah, come on.'"

"So, there was two state cars that came along with Jimmy. He brought them in case things got out of hand, I suppose. They didn't want to go in there, and they parked up and down the road from the juke joint. Leaving a trooper in each of the cars, Jimmy rode on in with me."

"Y'all were ready for whatever might happen, weren't you," Ellis interrupted, his interest gaining even though he had heard all this umpty times before. Carlton could tell a good story, and he kept on going.

"I said, 'We'll go in there and run 'em out.'"

"So, we went in there and I told the man in charge, 'You got to close the door because it's midnight on a Saturday night and they can't dance on Sunday. You're breaking the law and you got to close up. Right now!'"

"We locked up a whole cell full. We had so many in my car, I couldn't hardly drive. I had to put someone in the front with me to get 'em all to jail, which we did."

"So what happened to the ambush?" asked Ellis, bringing the story back to the original teaser line.

"You know, I never did find out for sure, but I expect it was all just tough talk with no real ambition behind it."

"Were you disappointed it went so peacefully?"

"Well, I'll admit maybe just a little bit." Carlton admitted. "But we sure closed that place down, and it didn't open the next weekend. I reckon we made an impression on them folks."

Sadly for them, the ambush didn't materialize that night, but Carlton could chalk up another juke joint righteously shut down for illegal Saturday night dancing. And, then there was their joint accident investigation, which did not end routinely. You just can't tell when the next good fight might come your way.

"But there was this other time, Ellis, when just the opposite happened. We thought we were workin' an ordinary traffic call, but it sure went south on us."

Ellis thought, could this be one I hadn't heard before?

"You see Jimmy had to cover a wreck there one day. He asked me, 'Do you want to go out there and help me with this wreck? Come on, go out with me.' So, I said, 'Sure.'"

"The wind was blowin' and it was so cold, just like today, and Jimmy got this man who caused the wreck and put him in the car where there wasn't no partition or nothing between the seats. So, the man was in the backseat while I was sitting up front. I said, 'I'll watch him while you go ahead and write it up. I'll be watching.'"

At this point, Ellis realized this was not a new story after all, but Carlton's way of telling it would be worth its repetition.

"When I was sitting there in that warm car that darn fella reached over the front seat and caught me around the neck. Boy, I sure hadn't seen that comin'!"

"When he surprised me as he did, I grabbed an old heavy-duty flashlight I'd put on the seat beside me, and, man, I peeled him upside the head and turned and jumped right on top of him in the back seat."

"And, then Jimmy came by and saw me sittin' on top of that man. He opened the door there and hit that fella on the jaw and knocked him cold as a cucumber. We came on in and locked him up. The next morning, the man told the Sheriff that I hit him and beat him up real bad. But I didn't hurt him, Jimmy is the one that hurt him. Sheriff carried him to the doctor, and he said, 'Carlton liked to kill me last night.'"

"Sheriff never did know that Jimmy was the one that hurt him. I got the blame for that. It liked to tickle Jimmy to death."

It amused Ellis, too, who was ready for more. He looked over to Beatrice Huff behind the counter, and called out to her, "How about some more coffee over here, Miz Huff. We're not quite ready to go back out in that cold."

She took the pot from the Bunn coffee maker and headed their way.

Calming down fights at juke joints was a continuing part of weekend police work. Carlton was almost as devoted to enforcing the Sunday blue laws as was Sheriff Wyatt in retiring moonshiners.

Carlton had just quelled a domestic dispute outside Siloam when his patrol car radio crackled and hissed at him.

"Carlton, you there?" it asked.

He took the mike off its hook on the dash. "Yep, go ahead," he answered.

"There's trouble over at the county work camp, Carlton. Some of the inmates are refusin' to work," said the dispatcher.

"Why are they doin' that?" Carlton asked knowing this had not happened before.

"Don't know, Carlton. Sheriff wants you to go over there and see what you can do."

"On my way," Carlton responded and re-hooked the mike.

He flipped on his roof-top lights in preparation for the turn he would make at Ronny Smith's Pure station up ahead. Then, heading back through Siloam, he took a small detour off the highway to drive by the house where he had just calmed down a seething and potentially murderous wife. He just wanted to make sure she hadn't changed her mind and gone forward with her previous intention of shot-gunning the bum.

Carlton cut off his flashers before he got to the residence where he slowed to see if there was a body out front. Nope. No body. But the car was gone. He smiled approvingly noting that she probably had taken his advice and gone to Atlanta to spend some time with her sister over there. With the lights turned back on and his foot pressed into the accelerator, Carlton resumed his route to the work camp.

Like many Georgia counties, Greene had a labor camp where low-risk prisoners were incarcerated and assigned to various labor tasks without pay. Road work was a common activity, and, for decades, gangs of prisoners had been chained together, overseen by rifle or shotgun-bearing guards, and sent out for a long-day of clearing shoulders of trash and roadkill, filling potholes, patching cracks with hot tar, and whatever else occurred to the supervisor that day. Although chain gangs were pretty much gone by this time,[14] county work camps, some of which persist to this very day, were common.

Greene's work camp, to which Carlton was headed, was run for the county by a contractor who employed guards and other staff to keep it operating smoothly. When he arrived, Carlton was met by the camp superintendent.

"Carlton, there's 16 or 17 men back in the main cell that won't come out to work. Can you go back there and get 'em to come on out?"

Rather than indignantly saying something like "Me? You want me to go bring out a bunch of prisoners on strike? Are you nuts?!," Carlton simply replied, "I'll get 'em out of there. Where are they?"

They entered the main structure where a substantial group of black prisoners was standing in a cluster in the back of a long cell. They were upright with arms folded across their chests – an image of staunch defiance if there ever was one. A force of heavily armed men stood outside the cell, and it was clear to Carlton that these guards had no intention whatsoever of going in after these men.

"Open the cell door," Carlton instructed the head guard, who quickly did as he was bid before stepping well back from the entrance. Carlton took off his holster belt and handed it to the superintendent before walking just inside the cell. He paused there. Many of the prisoners knew Carlton and his proclivity towards action, but they were still surprised at his willingness to take them on by himself while disarmed.

"You men get on out there and get to work," he ordered.

"No, Sir. We ain't!" one called out.

Another added, "They feedin' us garbage I wouldn't slop to my hogs."

"We sick and tired of them under-cooked and cold grits they give us all the time, Carlton," chimed in a third who Carlton remembered arresting after a juke joint fight a few months ago. A thought 'he's still here?' ran through his head.

"We not workin' no more from cain't see to cain't see[15] on the crap they givin' us, Carlton," was the next loud remark before the others started up a chorus of complaints over the poor food.

Carlton yelled, "HEY!," and even the guards were startled. The strikers grew quiet.

"Listen, men. I'm not here to negotiate over what they feed you. You are all in here 'cause the judge sentenced you to be here and work for the county until you are released. My one and only job is to make sure you obey the lawful sentence of the judge. You hearin' me!"

The chorus resumed with low mumbles that would soon crank back up to the litany of food complaints. There was no question in Carlton's mind that their complaints were valid, and he would talk with Sheriff Wyatt about that later, but only after these men went back to work. He was serious about enforcing the will of the court.

When he took a couple of steps in their direction, several men sucked in air, dropped their arms to their sides, and stepped towards him. The standoff was ramping up to something more.

Carlton would have none of it.

"I'm gonna have to come back there and get you!"

"Come on back!" the lead striker responded. The invitation was echoed by three or four others.

Carlton went on back.

The lead man came up to meet him, and, with no further hesitation or conversation Carlton grabbed him by the arm. They went at it after that, each slugging the other until Carlton got his arm around the man's neck to try to subdue him. The man responded by biting Carlton's arm and hand deep into the flesh. As the blood became apparent, a guard finally came in and pointed his gun at the biter saying he'd shoot him if he didn't stop. He and a few others who were considered the instigators were put in wrist and leg chains and led off to another cell. They would be transferred to a larger work prison serving nearby Augusta and Richmond County.

No one was badly injured, and Carlton would have walked away sore and bruised on his face had it not been for the arm and hand chomps. The emergency room physician doused the wounds in antiseptics, sewed him up, and gave him heavy-duty tetanus and antibiotic shots.[16] He also suspected that Carlton had a hairline fracture in a finger, so he packaged the whole bandaged-hand in a cast. Nothing could be done for the patient's swelling face, about which Carlton said nothing.

True to his word, Carlton told the Sheriff about the men's complaints over the work camp food. L. L. Wyatt acknowledged receipt of those complaints without saying whether or not the fare would improve.

Two weeks later, Carlton was called back to the camp. They were striking again for the same reason. A second set of ring leaders was transferred to Augusta.

Carlton also had to occasionally deal with escaped prisoners, an effort that usually employed dogs to find the escapees on the run. Carlton loved dogs and kept his own for coon hunting. That traditional Southern endeavor did not normally involve guns. It typically occupied an entire night sitting out in the boonies with your buddies by your vehicles and listening to your dogs when they located and then put a raccoon on the run or up a tree somewhere off in the distance. Each owner could identify a particular one of his dogs from its frantic barking tone and style. "That's old Blue way over yonder to the northwest," one might exclaim while another might counter with "No it ain't. That's my Jimbo. I'd recognize his coon voice any old time." They'd go back and forth on this important matter until the dogs would fall silent after the coon had, as usual, outwitted and escaped them. The men would return to talking politics and wives and telling tall tales and other lies to much laughter and bantering. Then the dogs would sound off after relocating that first coon or chancing on another. The conversation would revert to dog identification through the unique sound of each hound's hunting voice.

Although Carlton would not allow any alcohol whatsoever on his hunts, many would lubricate those long but pleasant nights with corn liquor made in the woods behind their house or bought just down the road from a neighbor. Come dawn, they'd pack up, with or without their dogs some of which wouldn't show up for a day or two – tired, filthy, loaded with fleas and ticks, and exhausted but eager to eat. Not uncommon would be some kind of wound inflicted by their intended prey or as a result of running through saw briars in the dark.

After adequate rest and recovery and a sufficient passage of time, both men and dogs would be eager for another all-night coon hunt. So, off they'd go well supplied with food, drink, and smokes, as well as a new stock of lies to laugh over during the night. The canine enthusiasm was even greater as they always forgot the misery of the following morning and that raccoons were typically smarter than them.

Carlton's devotion to coon hunting explained his enthusiasm about running the dogs who specialized in locating and chasing down escaped humans rather than four-legged creatures. In this case, though, humans and dogs hunted together as he was explaining to Ellis Buchanan one day.

"Ellis, I have to admit that when I was workin' for Sheriff Wyatt that I sure did enjoy running escaped convicts."

"I guess you don't get much of that now that you're Chief here do you?"

"No, almost never," Carlton responded wistfully.

"I remember one time when this man escaped out there from the work camp, and he'd been away half a day when, out of the blue, I saw him crossin' the road! I was in my car. I pulled on that side of the road where he was just jumping in the ditch. I yelled 'Stop!' And he stopped right there. I walked up to him and said, 'Let's go, you.'"

"I looked around after he just kind of looked over his shoulder like someone else was there. When I did, he came at me real quick like. I grabbed my pistol and I cocked it in his face. I brought him out of there, put the handcuffs on him, and brought him back to the work camp."

"So, he was trying to get the jump on you, huh? What would

you have done if he had?"

"Not worth thinkin' about, Judge, cause he didn't."

Ellis couldn't argue with that. Carlton had one more incident to relate.

"And another time I remember was at Reidsville[17] when three prisoners escaped. I think each one of them had about 40 years. We caught one that afternoon and one of them got away."

"We'd been running him with the dogs around midnight and all the rest of the searchers had quit, done give up 'cause we couldn't find him. I was driving slowly down this old road, and I heard this dog barking in a yard. I drove up in the yard. I got out of the car and I walked around the house – that old dog facing the house just barkin' his head off."

"I knew he saw somethin' he didn't much like by barking like that. I got down on my knees and looked under the house. And, there he was!"

"The fella's eyes were that big. I pulled my gun, and he said, 'Don't shoot, don't shoot.' The house was pretty close to the ground, so I reached in there and caught him by the hair of the head and pulled him out."

Ellis nodded approvingly and observed, "So a dog found that one anyway. Just wasn't one of your official blood hounds."

"That's right," Carlton agreed. "Bless them dogs, huh, Judge."

Ellis then asked Carlton, "That fella seemed pretty harmless. Were there dangerous criminals in those camps? I'd think you wouldn't want to risk one of them getting away."

"Now that you mention it. I remember one fella there from Atlanta who had life. He had a son who got killed. So, I went out to the camp and got him to take him to the funeral."

"I told him when we left, I said, 'Now listen, I'm bringing you up here, but don't get no ideas because you're going back to the farm with me.'"

"When we got over there to the house, I told him, 'I'll take you over there and let you see your boy, but I ain't going to stay over there at the funeral home all day long.'"

"After him seeing his dead boy, we come back by his house 'cause he was wanting to talk to his wife."

Ellis sensed something bad was about to be described to him. Carlton continued.

"She said, 'Let him come back here in the back room where we can talk privately.' I say, 'Well, you can go, but I'm going with you.' So, I went in the back room with him, and she got crazy! She didn't care if I was in there or not. She just jumped on him and started cussing and everything."

"I saw he was kind of getting mad himself, so I said, 'Come on, let's go.' I just took him on out. As soon as we got in the car he said, 'Carlton, I'm glad you brought me out cause I'd a killed that heifer.'"

"Now, I had thought he was starting to get mad, but not that mad. I carried him on back down there to the farm. That was part of our job, to work with the prisoners on family things like that. You never knew how it would turn out, but you'd better be ready for anything."

Chap 4 — Illicit Booze and Dangerous Boozers

Sheriff L. L. Wyatt had a passion for putting Greene County's outsized number of bootleggers out of business and behind bars. This determination commenced with his 1925 hiring by the Greene County Commission as a special policeman with that one particular mission. Wyatt's predecessor as sheriff only occasionally raided a still for show and blatantly operated a small distillery in his own front yard for personal consumption. For fifteen years, Wyatt would destroy countless stills and pour an ocean of Greene's renowned hooch into the soil where cotton had flourished before the boll weevil showed up. Wyatt felt it his divine calling to eliminate the scourge of alcohol from Greene County, and he would have accomplished this mission had there not been other moonshiners ready to step in as soon as he retired the current crop of deep-woods distillers. Atlanta's demand for whiskey, and the price paid for it, only increased as the suppliers diminished. When Wyatt became Sheriff in 1940, he had other responsibilities on top of his continued vigilance against illegal whiskey, but illegal liquor producers were always on his mind.

Carlton Lewis shared Wyatt's deep religious faith as well as the Sheriff's teetotaling lifestyle, but he lacked the intense focus on moonshining of the man who first hired him into law enforcement. There were other crimes, he felt, that more adversely affected the citizens he was sworn to protect. Nevertheless, moonshiners were criminals Carlton would go after when they came to his attention. As an offshoot of his love of hunting, he really liked going out and looking for stills hidden in the forests.

Those hunts usually followed tipoffs from a system of informants who provided an especially fruitful return on Sheriff

Wyatt's investment in a web of open-eyed folks scattered throughout his Greene domain. There was never a shortage of stills to raid or liquor runners to chase down throughout the county, hitting the backroads to Atlanta at high speed and even higher profits. Carlton loved the excitement of these hunts and locked up many of his prey.

The biggest still they got out of these tips was located right outside of Greensboro, almost in plain sight rather than in some tree-hidden hollow. This one had an impressive amount of sugar stockpiled to feed a boiler that was as big as a steam sawmill's.

The visionary liquor entrepreneurs for this impressive contraption had run a power cable up from a house to the still. They had also run a water line down to a branch to pump the fine, clear water up to the whiskey site. They had everything they needed, except, of course, a license to manufacture distilled spirits. Most moonshiners set up alongside their water source, so this innovative way around that requirement made the production site hard to find. But, as usual, the Sheriff's Office got a little tip about this one, and Carlton and his favorite federal revenue agent, Lanny Ferguson, went out looking for it.

"Carlton, you need to get your snitches to give you better information as to the whereabouts of these things. This one could be in South Carolina for all we know," Lanny bellyached.

"Oh, get over it, Lanny. We'll find this fella soon enough. Just lean back and enjoy the hunt. Okay?" Carlton took the next turn off the road as the informant had instructed, and sure enough, there was a house with a big wooded hill behind it.

"Well, if this is the place, these boys are sure breaking tradition," Carlton offered.

"What ya mean?" Lanny responded.

"This place is barely two miles out of Greensboro right under our noses. That's downright brash if you ask me," was Carlton's reply.

"Ifff," Lanny drew out the word for emphasis, "this is the right place."

"All right now, let's go take a look."

While Lanny went around to the back of the house, Carlton climbed to the porch where he opened the screen door and knocked loudly.

Nothing – so he knocked again, even more loudly.

Lanny was rounding the side of the house as Carlton stepped down from the porch.

"Nobody home, my friend," Lanny opined. "I peaked in a bunch of windows and it don't look like nobody's livin' there right now. Even the icebox is propped open with a chair. What you wanna do, buddy?"

Carlton went back up on the porch and peered into a couple of windows.

"I do believe you stumbled on the truth here, Lanny."

"What you mean 'stumbled?'"

"There ain't no furniture in the livin' room, and the big ole mattress in that front bedroom is bare – no sheets, no pillows, no nuthin'. Let's take a walk up that hill back there," Carlton suggested.

"You da boss, Carlton. Lead the way." Lanny bent from the waist and waved his hand like a head waiter indicating an open table.

Carlton just shook his head and headed up hill. Along the way, he noticed a line of disturbed dirt that had been covered in pine straw. He stopped and looked at Lanny, pointing at it.

Lanny reacted with, "Yeah, I saw that, too. Looks pretty fresh, don't it?" Carlton nodded in agreement, turned and resumed the climb.

The hill was treed over and level on top. They looked back down at the quiet and abandoned house and listened for any approaching traffic – nothing but birds and the wind.

They both drew their revolvers, and slowly entered the woods. It wasn't fifty feet until they came up on it – the biggest still either one of them had ever seen – and it was cooking away.

Now, this is where the situation can head south quickly, and they both knew it. There might be three operators just off in the woods with shotguns trained on them and burial sites all set to go.

"Lanny," Carlton whispered, "Let's go back down to the house and look inside. There was lots of inner rooms we didn't see. I bet they got some stored there. We'll call back and get some help here as well."

Lanny nodded his concurrence, and they backed away from the site and headed downhill. They stopped by the car first to get more firepower and then make that radio call to the sheriff's office which was only about ten minutes away. Two more deputies would be there soon, and the State Patrol would be on the way over from Madison.

They flipped a coin and Lanny won. So, he reared back and kicked open the front door. They'd post-date a search warrant later if needed.

It was an old shotgun style farm house with rooms off each side of the long, central hallway. The dining room was piled high with half-bushel bags of corn and 20-pound bags of sugar. Two bedrooms were brimming with filled gallon jugs numbering in the hundreds. Another bedroom was full of empties awaiting the firewater now cooking away up the hill.

"I'll bet them boys went away to stretch their legs a while and will come back sooner or later when it's time for a bottling run. It occurs to me that we'd better be hid out rather than have our little army in plain sight down here."

"I agree, Carlton, you'd better go out and call off our incoming dogs. We'll get your car tucked away somewhere and find a hidey hole up the hill to watch our liquor-making friends come back."

Fifteen minutes later, they were hidden in the woods at the top of the hill on its opposite side from the house, their car out of site on a dead-end fire road that showed no recent tire ruts. One of them could get to the car's radio in about five minutes to call their reinforcements back in. They got down in the thick brush not knowing how long their wait would be. Lanny had an old Winchester Model 1876 carbine made popular by Teddy Roosevelt that could literally kill an elephant and Carlton had his sawed-off 12-gauge. They also each had two sticks of dynamite that would disintegrate the still at the appropriate time or serve as hand grenades if necessary.

They were set for anything, including the patience needed for the long wait, not knowing when, or even if, the moonshiners would come to check on their still.

An hour passed, and it was still just them, the birds, and the wind. Lanny got a hankering for a cigarette, but he knew its smell could alert incomers. So, he fought back the nicotine craving. Then a second hour snailed by.

Well into the third hour, they both heard the sound of snapping twigs. Soon, a man came out of the woods opposite the still from them whistling softly to himself. He was carrying a paper sack but otherwise appeared to be unarmed, at least of any long guns. He looked around briefly, confirmed that whiskey was still dripping out the distilled end and sat down on a camp stool. He reached into his back pocket and pulled out a half-pint of amber liquid that he uncorked to toss back a dose. It was pretty standard that moonshiners bought legal whiskey. Maybe it was a superstition, but their product was for them to sell, not to drink. The man then produced a sandwich from the sack and contentedly lit into a late lunch.

That was it. Nobody else was with him.

They knew he couldn't handle this all by himself, so they just settled back in to continue the wait for more hands to show up on deck.

It wasn't half an hour until a voice called out from the other side of the hill.

"Hey, Butch! You up there? Can you hear me, Butch?"

Butch could hear him, alright, as could Carlton and Lanny and anybody else within a quarter mile.

"That you, Gene? I'm here. Everything's lookin' just fine!" Butch called back.

"Good," Gene hollered. "John and M. Z. will be here in about ten minutes."

Gene reached the top of the hill and the conversation dropped into lower tones. The hidden police officers were downright shocked about the lack of security these clowns were employing, yelling off through the woods like that.

Carlton mimicked picking up a microphone. Lanny nodded, and the deputy eased back on hands and knees and then went on down to the cruiser to call in the troops. In ten minutes, it would be six heavily armed policemen against four doofus moonshiners. Should be no contest.

Just as Carlton settled back into position, Butch got up and brushed sandwich crumbs off his hands. "Back in a minute," he announced to his colleague, "nature's callin'." Butch went around the still from where he was sitting and headed straight towards the onlookers. He stopped, dropped his pants, and squatted not fifteen feet from Carlton, now scrunched deep into the ground cover.

His business finished, Butch zipped up his pants, took a pack of Camels from his shirt pocket, and walked off to rejoin Gene, whose attention was then fully engaged by the contents of his own paper sack. They both were soon on the ground for a good nap.

Carlton looked over at Lanny, giving him a can-you-believe-that look when they both turned toward the sound of the approach of the additional deputies and troopers. They were appropriately stealthy, but a pipe and drum corps likely wouldn't have roused their quarry. The four new officers spread out to form a half perimeter using hand signals from Carlton. Then the six waited for the others to arrive at the still.

Twenty minutes later, Butch, Gene, John, and M. Z. sat crossed-legged on the ground, their hands cuffed behind them. Two others were in custody on the front porch of the house. None of the prisoners had been armed or offered any resistance at the surprise raid. They were subdued and depressed at the ease with which all their labors had suddenly come to nothing except for the prospect of big fines and some jail time.

Sheriff L. L. Wyatt with deputies Reese Smith and Carlton Lewis at a still brought in to Greensboro for display by the old county jail.

The next day, under the headline "6 arrested in Greene Still raid," *The Herald-Journal* reported that "Greene County Deputy Sheriff Carlton Lewis" said that five men were arrested at a still with 2,800 gallons of illegal liquor all set for bottling. Another moonshiner had been taken into custody at a house where 2,000 gallons of their product was already bottled and ready for shipment. The still, which could produce about 500 gallons a day, had only been operating for about two weeks before the raid. An accompany photo of the operation appeared under the prominent caption "LAW OFFICERS RAID GIANT WHISKEY STILL IN OPERATION."

Carlton, who had been heartily congratulated by Sheriff Wyatt, told everyone how pleased he was with the raid. But only to a few of his closest friends did he relate his disappointment that none of those six guys had tried to resist arrest.

Carlton would occasionally be gone for several days tucked away with a couple of ATF officers in the woods next to a still awaiting the arrival of its operators. To the hunter in Carlton, it was like sitting in a camouflaged deer stand waiting for that 15-point buck to come sidling by with the exception that Carlton might be in his moonshiner stand for two or three days.

Eleanor and Tom would hear nothing from Carlton until it was over and Carlton had bagged the moonshiners and confiscated their product for evidence. Tom came home from basketball practice one afternoon to discover fifty or more gallon-jugs of moonshine lined up in the carport. His father had hauled in the hooch for evidence against the unlucky targets of his latest hunt. Tom would see a stash like this on another couple of occasions.

L. L. Wyatt would heartily endorse this area of policing, but he would have been disappointed after Carlton became a police chief and paid less attention to locking up moonshiners and more to the safety of the citizens he swore to protect.

Moonshine is still made in Georgia, although rarely illegally. Instead, there are a growing number of licensed, small-batch distilleries that feature fine, barrel-aged bourbons, ryes, rums, flavored vodkas and gins as well as unaged and water-clear whiskey, aka moonshine. One wonders, though, if L. L. could resist carrying a big axe with him if he walked into, say, the perfectly legal Dawsonville Moonshine Distillery today.

Of course, it was not just the illegal whisky that was a problem.

In the long run, more serious was the wreckage left in the paths of incorrigible drunks on the road, in bars, and in their own homes. On a weekend trip home from college, Tom recalls that he and his parents were finishing dinner when the phone rang. The dispatcher told Carlton a call had come in on a drunk white man who was beating up some black men out in the country. Could Carlton please go out and stop this fellow from abusing folks?

"Come on, Tommy. Go with me. You can drive the guy's car back home while I take him in," the Chief more than asked his son.

So, they got into the police car and headed out to cool the situation down. The dispatcher had identified the miscreant as a man named Ray.[18] Carlton knew right away who they were talking about as Ray was employed by the county as a heavy equipment operator. Tommy had gone to school with his son. Ray, a big man weighing in at 250 or so, was apparently in his cups that evening when something ticked him off and he took it out on some black citizens. They had good reason to fear for their physical well-being with this riled-up and drunken giant of a white man.

When they got there, Ray was sitting on a stump, staring out into the woods. Carlton walked up to him.

"Come on, Ray, let's go. You can't behave like this beating up innocent people."

Ray stood and approached Carlton, putting an outstretched hand on each of the Chief's shoulder. He was a head taller than Carlton who didn't try to step back or brush away Ray's grip.

"Take your durn hands off me," Carlton said slowly.

"I'm gonna teach you a lesson. I'm gonna whip your ass," he informed the policeman.

"Like Hell, you are," Carlton replied while stepping back and cocking his right arm.

When his chin caught the blow, Ray hit the ground like a stunned water buffalo.

"Come over here, Tommy, and help me get Ray in the car."

Getting his senses back as they lugged him to the cruiser to be stuffed into the back seat, a now docile Ray looked at Tommy as if seeking his sympathy and said, "Your daddy slapped the shit out of me."

Chap 5 — Failure to Maintain Lane

Approaching Greensboro on I-20

The Reverend Hosea Lorenzo Williams, known as "Hosie" to many who loved him for what he stood for while forgiving him of his sins, was committing one of those transgressions by driving erratically on I-20 well east of Atlanta. His fame for collecting and subsequently slipping out of DUIs and other traffic driving violations was legendary.[19] He was about to add to that remarkable record.

Sheriff's Deputy Lewis was descending the merging ramp onto interstate from the Rutledge exit when a Cadillac sailed by on the freeway well under the speed limit but badly weaving in and out of its lane. Carlton sighed, lit up his lights and advanced to pull yet another drunk driver off the road who he would shove into the sobering legal gauntlet that lay ahead. He almost felt sorry for the guy until he thought of the havoc he could wreak for all those innocents obeying the law while driving on this freeway.

Carlton was up behind the car quickly, red lights flashing brilliantly, but the driver kept on plugging along, most likely trying to show his interceptor that he could indeed drive inside the lane markers. Wrong. He couldn't.

Impatient to get this guy off the road, Carlton toggled on his siren. He could see the fellow repeatedly glancing into his rear-view mirror until it dawned on him that he should pull over. He fulfilled that realization by breaking way too fast, something Carlton had anticipated, and jerked the Caddy to a stop on the shoulder.

As Carlton chunked his door shut, he instinctively patted his holstered service revolver, memorized the man's license plate number, and strolled with suitable wariness to the driver's side window, already rolled down.

"Sir, do you know why I stopped you?" he asked.

"Yes sir, Officer, I believe I do. And do you, sir, know who I am?" the man slurred with a tolerant smile on his face.

"Yes, Reverend, I believe I do, but why don't you hand me your driver's license just to be sure I'm on the right track."

"And, why do you need my license, Officer, if you know who I am?"

"Well, Sir, this here form I'm filling out requires that I write in your name, spelled correctly, your license number, and your address before I arrest you and put you in the back seat of that car there behind you."

Anticipating a yokel cop, Hosea recalibrated his take on the situation and handed over the license with a big smile.

Glancing at the license for confirmation of the identity of this man, Carlton continued, "Welcome to Greene County, Reverend Williams. Sheriff Wyatt will be delighted to meet you."

"Well, Officer – or is it Deputy – I'm all yours. Let's go talk to your famous Sheriff Wyatt who will no doubt be proud to decorate his jail with a man of my stature."

With Hosea Williams deposited without handcuffing in the back seat, he and Carlton chatted amiably until a wrecker arrived to haul off the Cadillac to the impound yard.

Then, they were off to Greensboro and a visit with L. L. Wyatt.

L. L. Wyatt made Greene County tick like a precision timepiece. While he was officially the county's elected Sheriff, he was unofficially and for all intents and purposes the political leader of the entire domain of Greene. Nothing of significance happened in any corner of the county without being reported to him by one of his snitches stationed in each of the county's districts. Any seeker of any office at any level came to L. L. for his blessing with the knowledge that without it there would be no appointment nor election to the desired post.

If there ever was such a thing as a benevolent dictator, it was L. L. Wyatt. He was a fair man, and he taught the staff and officers of his small law enforcement department to treat all whom they encountered with impartiality and respect tempered with firmness.

While Wyatt could pretty much control all that took place from within his county, he could not control what might enter from the outside. Of particular concern was the possibility of civil rights demonstrations such as those that had occurred in neighboring Crawfordville, seat of tiny Taliaferro County whose population was a fraction of Greene's but whose ill-planned schemes for avoiding school desegregation in 1965 made them front-page news nationally for months. Greene County had assisted their neighbors in "Tolliver," as Taliaferro is pronounced in Georgia, by taking some of their white students when the county closed down the white school to keep it from being integrated.

Weeks of student protests in Crawfordville were amplified manyfold in significance when Martin Luther King's Southern Christian Leadership Conference decided to join the protests and make an example of the county's cynicism and hypocrisy in its pretense to abide by the Civil Rights Act of 1964. King asked his lieutenant Hosea Williams to participate in amplifying the demonstrations, which was essentially Williams' job description within the SCLC. He was very good at his job. The Taliaferro school system was put under federal court control and integration was ordered. The minority white population responded by putting most of the white children into private academies, which were then in vogue as the latest means for thwarting integration orders. The county schools were thereby all black with some 90 additional black kids ordered into the systems of those counties that, as had Greene, connived with their neighbor to ward off integration.[20]

Greene County, in which Eleanor Lewis was a teacher,

subsequently set out to become an example of compliance, but the county's complicity with Taliaferro made them vulnerable to demonstrations for past offenses. One of L. L. Wyatt's great concerns was to see Hosea Williams coming into Greene County bent on punishment.

Thus, one can only imagine Wyatt's reaction when Deputy Sheriff Carlton Lewis arrived in Greensboro to book Rev. Williams for driving while intoxicated. The wheels must have spun rapidly in the Sheriff's mind concerning the predicament his latest prisoner was in. Here, he thought, was an external situation now under his control.

Following introductions, the Sheriff asked the Reverend and his deputy to step into his office. Carlton was invited to describe how he came to pull over the prisoner, which Carlton did, and Wyatt turned to Williams.

"Reverend, is what Deputy Lewis just stated accurate?"

"I believe, Sheriff Wyatt, that what he just related is generally truthful," Williams acknowledged.

"Well, Sir, you must understand that drunk driving is a very serious offense that the Greene County Superior Court punishes with appropriate severity. Consequently, a large fraction of our county work farm inmates has been sentenced there as a result of their disregard of the scourge of man's sinful enamoration of alcohol."

Wyatt paused for a reaction.

"I understand what you are saying, Sheriff."

Another long pause without loss of eye contact.

"You are a very important man, Reverend Williams, with important work that must be carried forward to ensure that the South proceeds as it should into compliance with the law of the land."

Williams acknowledged the accuracy of that statement with a slow nod of courtesy. Wyatt continued.

"I can ask Deputy Lewis to tear up that DUI citation right here and now, but there is a condition, a simple one." Although accustomed to having charges like this dropped, the presence of an underlying condition was intriguing. Without speaking, Williams tilted his head and raised his eyebrows in question.

"Your arrest will be vacated and kept quiet if you agree to never target Greene County for any civil rights action or demonstration. I must have your word on that, Sir."

Hosea Williams stood and stretched out his right hand. "You have my word on your condition, Sheriff. I know the good work you and your county leaders here in Greene do for your Negro citizens. Dr. King is aware of that as well."

Wyatt stood and took Williams' hand before turning to his deputy.

"Carlton, please allow Reverend Williams to call someone to come pick him up and then take him for a meal and coffee while he waits for them to drive over from Atlanta."

"Yes sir," replied Carlton as he nodded to his former prisoner. "This way, Reverend."

As they approached the door to take leave of Wyatt's office, Williams paused and turned back to the man now sitting stiffly at his desk, hands stretched out with palms flat on the table top.

"Is there something more, Reverend?" Wyatt asked.

Williams took a good three-second look at the Sheriff while making a real-time decision.

"No, Sheriff. It was a pleasure meeting you."

Wyatt stood up. "The pleasure was all mine, Reverend."

L. L. Wyatt and Hosea Williams never met again.

Hosea Williams took another bite from a mound of three scrambled eggs and washed it down with a generous sip of very hot coffee. He was about to fork up some of the sausage when he changed his mind and looked over at Carlton.

"That sheriff of yours is a real piece of work, isn't he?"

"Why, yes, just as most folks would say that about you, too."

"Really?" Williams feigned indignation and then grinned. "The world can only stand so many of us, don't you think?"

"We all have our special roles, Reverend. The Lord assigns those to us at birth."

"Yes, indeed, Deputy, and He certainly gave you a special role in this little negotiation, didn't He?"

"I don't follow you, Reverend," Carlton replied with a twinkle in his eye."

"Well, you could have tossed me in a cell and filed charges just as you would normally do to an unfortunate soul like me caught in such circumstances. But, you didn't."

"I figured the Sheriff would be honored to meet you, Sir."

Williams looked intently at Carlton over the top of the glasses he had put on to get a better view of his plate and then grinned before returning his attention to his fork and that sausage patty.

William's decision not to have that final word with Sheriff Wyatt had suddenly seemed pointless. Surely this God-fearing sheriff knew perfectly well that he and the SCLC had no intention of launching civil rights actions against Greene County. Greene wasn't perfect, of course, but it was a far cry from other locales in Georgia and throughout the South where egregious racial injustice screamed for active response. The ministers of Greene County's black churches were not unhappy with what they anticipated would be their community's response to new federal laws, and the area had already received considerable attention in the media from the activities in Taliaferro County subsequently summed up by a Georgia social-justice activist when she said, "If Taliaferro County used as much ingenuity in educating children as in evading the civil rights law, it would have the greatest school system in the state."[21] The condition Wyatt had put on his release was not a bargaining chip, it was a Get-Out-of-Jail-Free card handed him by a man with a good heart.

Did L. L. and Carlton know about Williams' experience in World War II? That he fought as an enlisted man in a colored unit in Patton's Third Army in which he made it to staff sergeant. That he was seriously wounded in a Luftwaffe bomb attack that killed thirteen of his fellow soldiers. That he spent a year in an English hospital recuperating before returning home to Georgia. That upon his return home, and while in uniform, he was nearly beaten to death during a long delay in the Americus, Georgia bus station for taking a drink from a water fountain.[22]

'Oh, well,' Williams said to himself, 'I'll take it,' and went off for that meal and some conversation with the deputy who had done his duty but who had taken him to see the famous L. L. Wyatt rather than lock him in a cell like any other drunk driver.

While Hosea Williams drove through the county on I-20 numerous times, he never stopped there. Likely as not, though, he thought of his brief interlude with that county's Sheriff's department.

But, this was not to be the last time he would interact in a critical situation with a Greene County Lewis.

One of those locales with astonishingly overt racial intolerance was Forsyth County whose seat at Cumming is some 40 miles north-northeast of Atlanta. Forsyth's segregationist story is too long and complex to recount here,[23] but the infamous road sign that read "*Nigger, don't let the Sun set on you in Forsyth County*" says it all. People heeded that sign, and by 1980 only one African American was known to live in Forsyth.

On January 17, 1987, Williams led a march of about 75 blacks and whites outside of Cumming setting the courthouse there as their destination. They carried signs like "*Give Brotherhood a Chance*" to which the counter-demonstrators responded with "*Sickle-Cell*

Anemia – the Great White Hope." Rocks were thrown at Williams' protestors – one striking Williams himself in the head. Bruised and bleeding, the demonstrators fled Forsyth. The Ku Klux Klan declared it a great triumph. Maybe so, but it was short-lived.[24]

Seven days later, some 20,000 marchers and prominent activists, including Jesse Jackson and Coretta Scott King, converged on Forsyth along with state and national politicians. Governor Joe Frank Harris was determined that this march would have adequate protection and not be a repeat on a vast scale of Hosea Williams' first Forsyth march.

The Governor sent his chief of staff, Tom Lewis – Carlton's son – to supervise security for the March. The Georgia National Guard, the GBI, and the Georgia State Patrol were out in full force. Tom knew it was the state's duty and obligation to carry out the Governor's orders that the protestors be protected. A long program of speakers was in the outing, and Tom feared that things would get out of control with the descent of January's early darkness. There with Tom in the command post at the Forsyth County courthouse was Atlanta Mayor Andrew Young. Lewis discussed his concern with Young, and they set the goal of ending all the speeches, including one by Hosea Williams, well before dark. The Mayor would serve as master of ceremonies with the primary job of getting the speakers to and then away from the microphone as quickly as possible. Otherwise, many would linger there, and darkness would settle in. Young performed masterfully to fulfill Tom Lewis' goal, and the huge demonstration ended peacefully.[25]

Carlton did not see this second Lewis-Williams interaction – he had died ten months prior to the Forsyth marches.

Chap 6 — Grabbing Shotguns & Other Close Calls

The car sped right by a city cop in Greensboro.

"This guy's ripe for a hefty ticket," the officer mumbled to no one, lit up his flashers and took after the speeder. To his surprise, the car did not just slow down and pull over as is conventionally done. In fact, it sped up and was high-tailing it out of town. The siren was then added to the flashing lights to convey urgency but to no effect. Then the man slowed as if to pull over. Instead, he made a sharp turn onto an unpaved road and kicked up the pace again. Rocks and dust spewed back at the police car as the chase continued.

At this point, the officer called into home base to report the situation and was told to keep them posted. As he sat the mike on the seat cushion beside him, the man swerved into a long driveway, obviously heading to the old house at the top of the hill. He did a skidding stop, flung open his door, and ran toward the house. In his right hand was a pump action shotgun.

Jerking the mike up off the seat, a heart-thumping officer reported a situation that had suddenly taken a very unpleasant turn.

"Sit tight, Arnie, ya hear," he was told. "I'll call the county and state and get some help out there for you."

No worries about him not sitting tight. He wasn't going anywhere near that house. He retrieved his own shotgun, bolted out of the car, and squatted behind it to get some steel between himself and that other guy's buckshot.

Carlton was just about to leave home to go on patrol when his phone rang.

"This is Carlton," he answered.

"Hey, Carlton," the county dispatcher said, "Arnie's got a feller holed up in the man's house with a shotgun. He needs some help. Can you go out there and maybe flush 'im out for ole Arnie."

"Sure can. Where they at?"

Carlton knew the address as he'd been there once or twice before. He concluded that City Arnie must have chased this rabbit down his hole for some infraction in Greensboro.

When he got to his car, Carlton checked the load in his shotgun to make sure it was back to double-ought instead of the birdshot he'd used dove hunting last weekend. Buckshot it was.

When he arrived at the house, Carlton saw several more police cars already there – two state and one other Greensboro city officers had beat him to the scene. The other city cop had joined Arnie on the ground behind his car while the two from the state patrol were ensconced behind an outbuilding. Presumably the man was still in the house with the gun. Carlton pulled up beside Arnie's vehicle, and called out to the city boys.

"Well, how the devil y'all going to get him standing out here? You got to go in there and get him. You can't get him from out here!"

"If we go in there, he'll shoot us for sure!" Arnie responded, explaining the obvious.

Carlton sighed in disgust and took off in a zig-zag run up to the carport, astonishing his three fellow officers with such suicidal rashness.

He could see the man through the carport entry door's window. He was standing by the kitchen table, shotgun in his right hand, with a dazed look as if wondering what the Hell he'd do next. Carlton snatched the man from his reverie by knocking loudly on the door.

"Come on out here!"

"No!" the startled man responded.

"Well, then, I'm comin' in! You better get set 'cause I'm comin' in to get you!"

Midway through the man's reply of "You better not come in

here," Carlton kicked the door open, went in fast and grabbed the man's arm yanking the shotgun from his grip.

"Now get on out there like I told you!"

When they got in the carport, the man decided to put up a fight, stomping on Carlton's toe in the process. At this point – after Carlton had disarmed the miscreant and got him outside – all the other police officers came running up from their positions of safety and helped Carlton load up the enraged speeder, now a felon, into his police cruiser.

Walking up to a potentially deranged man and disarming him of his shotgun is something you would think an officer would only do once before coming to his senses.

Carlton and Ellis had just paid their lunch tabs when the Union Point Police Chief had an inspiration.

"Say, Judge, I'm going to walk up through town to do my usual drop-ins on the business folks to make sure all's okay. Why don't you come along with me?"

"You serious?" Ellis asked doubtfully.

"Sure am. You'd like seeing your old constituents, wouldn't you? Besides, the exercise would be good for ya, and the store owners would enjoy seeing you. Come on along with me. You can pull away any time if you get tired or bored. You got a few years on me and might need to rest."

That did the trick.

"What?" Ellis asked indignantly. "I won't need rest any more than you would. Let's go."

The two jaywalked Lamb Avenue to head up Scott. Carlton wanted to stop by City Hall for any messages before going on his rounds. On the way up there, he started a sequel to the Arnie rescue story.

"You know, Judge, that wasn't the only time I took a gun away from a man," Carlton admitted.

"Why does that not surprise me. You've got the guts of an entire infantry brigade."

Carlton laughed and replied, "Hey, now, remember I'm a Navy man."

"I stand corrected. Now, go ahead and tell me the story."

"Okay. There was this fella John. He was a real nutcase. When he'd get to drinking he'd get really crazy. John and his brother Rowen lived next door to each other, and John would get after him with a gun. I had to go down there several times to calm things down. One time it was because John was drunk and shooting over at his brother's house with a shotgun from his front porch."

"You know, I think those two were in my court once, fighting over some stupid thing or another, but I forget. Go on."

They got to City Hall.

"Take five, Judge. Smoke 'em if you got 'em. Be right back."

Ellis sighed but said nothing. True to his word, Carlton was soon back.

"Alright, now they know where I'm heading. We'll go up the alley here for the back way to the bank."

He resumed the story.

"So, I got there and went up to Rowen who told me what happened. I said, 'Well, I'll go down there and talk to him.' He said, 'Okay, I'll go with you.' I said, 'If I was you, I wouldn't do that.' He told me it'd be alright, so I told him 'Well, come on then.'"

"I walked over to John's house with Rowen following me. John was on his porch with the shotgun and drunk as a skunk. He saw Rowen and told him 'If you come over here, I am going to shoot you,' he said, 'I am going to shoot your ass off!' So, ole Rowen turns around and goes home."

"At least someone has made a rational decision," Ellis noted.

"I get your gist, Judge. Anyway, here's the bank."

They went in. Carlton stopped at both teller stations to say hello and ask if they needed anything. One thing no one did at the

Farmers Bank was to joke about a robbery. Reuben Flynt would always be in the back of bank employees minds, even if they hadn't worked there that fateful December day in 1975. Two customers waiting to talk to a bank officer about their business got up and came to pay their respects to Judge Buchanan, who was clearly pleased by their recognizing him.

By the time they had both gone back to say hello to the bank president, fifteen minutes had passed at which point Carlton announced, "We'd best be on our rounds. Doc Rhodes is the next stop. So, where was I, Judge."

"Rowen made the right decision to go home," Ellis stated in an attempt to reiterate his point.

"Oh, yeah. Well, that left me and John with him standing on his porch, drunk and with that shotgun. I said, 'John let me talk to you.' 'I don't want to talk to you, Carlton. I am going to shoot you. Don't you come up here.' I was just talking and taking a few steps. He raised the gun on me again and when he'd raise the gun, I'd stop. I'd get to talking to him, and I'd take a few more steps. Then he'd raise that gun on me again. He raised that thing on me about four times. Finally, I got close enough to him, and I reached and got hold of that gun by the barrel. I snatched it out of his hand, grabbed him and then threw his butt in the car and took him to lock him up."

"A few nights after he'd been let out, John, of course, had it in for me. He went completely wild down there. He was running down through the woods by his house with a shotgun and hollering, 'There goes Carlton Lewis!' And, he'd fire that gun. BOOM! And, he'd holler some more about me and fire it off again. BOOM!"

"The Sheriff called me and said, 'Don't you dare come down there. I'll have somebody get John.' They finally got him that night and took him off to Milledgeville, and he's been in and out of the state hospital ever since."

"Here we are. Let's see if the Doc's in or out on a house call," said Carlton as he opened the door for Ellis.

"Daddy, you gotta be crazy to do something like that," Tom Lewis later admonished his father. "I know it really put Mother beside herself that you'd go up to a man with a shotgun and just take it from him. And, then the second time around it was with a mental patient! What were you thinking? Weren't you scared?"

"You know, Tommy, a situation like that doesn't really scare me that much. But, when its domestic – that's when you know you are going to get hurt. That's when you know you're in trouble."

"Why's that, Dad?"

"Well, you see, you get this woman whose husband is knocking her around. So, she calls us for help and we go out there to keep him from really bashing her. In the process, he puts up a fight, so we have to knock 'im in the head. At this point, she goes nuts and comes after you with both hands. Then you got to fight 'em both. You got to fight everybody in the house. When you first got there, you're the cavalry coming to the rescue. Then, things spin around on a dime, and you're the devil. Now, that's what's dangerous. I'd take that fella with the shotgun anytime."

Carlton was a right. Nearly a quarter of all line of duty deaths of police officers occur while responding to domestic violence calls.[26] It turns out that car accidents nationally result in more officer deaths than domestic situations. But, you are more likely to get shot on a domestic call by someone in an extremely agitated state of mind than in an armed robbery situation. Carlton did not learn this in a criminal justice class. He discovered this fact first hand.

Still, that knowledge was insufficient to curtail his audacity in confronting a man with a gun who had just committed a serious offense against a woman. Here is Carlton's telling of a case in point. It was yet another disarming a man initiative that he hadn't told Ellis or Tom. He also expressed his expectations for a real policeman.

"Nowadays, when there's a domestic involving a man with a gun, the police just get a bunch of men together and go out there to wait it out. Just like when old Isaac Mitchell got mad and shot his girlfriend.

"They sent two men up there and then called for another county man. They said Isaac was in the house with a gun and they was walking out there in the road, doin' nothin'. Maybe send some gas down here to get him out was all they could think of.

"They called me, and I went up there. I said, 'Where's the man?'

"'Ah, he's in the house,' they told me.

"So, I just walked around the house and there he was out there sitting on the back steps with a gun beside him while those police were all sitting out front with all their guns.

"I told Isaac, 'Don't you put your hand on that gun.'

"I walked up there and reached up and got it. Then, I said, 'Come on.' He got up and walked out of there and got in my truck.

"You don't call them boys standing around out front policemen."

It is hard to argue against Carlton's point except to realize that if all policemen had to be like him, we would have a serious shortage of police officers on this planet.

The call came in from a woman about her husband being drunk and getting mad at her like he always did. "I'm afraid he's gonna start punchin' on me like he's done before. I just cain't take no more of that. Can y'all come out here and help me?"

The dispatcher "yes ma'amed" her and called the Chief.

"All right. I'll head on by there to see what's goin' on. Let me know if she calls back."

Carlton had an old black policeman with him who was doing some part-time work. When they arrived at the house, Carlton sighed as he got out of the car and passingly wondered if Eleanor was right about him getting too old for this kind of stuff. Walking into a house heated up with family passions like this was like going into a pit of vipers. You never knew which one might bite you.

Carlton knocked once when they got to the front door.

"Police!" he announced, "I'm comin' on in!" The old policeman stayed by the door while Carlton entered.

It was clear that the man and his wife had been hard at it, but the man was sitting on the sofa at this point. His wife was standing off at the side, breathing heavily and looking at her husband with an untempered loathing. Carlton's danger warning went up another notch, and he knew he'd better get the man out of there pronto.

"Get up, now," he said to the man. "I'm takin' you in."

"No, you ain't," was the response, delivered through gritted teeth, "I ain't goin' nowhere. You don't have no bidness comin' into my house. Get on back out!"

So, Carlton did what he had to do. He grabbed the man's arm and jerked him from the couch. He rammed the arm behind the man, while putting his own free arm around his waist and started to frogmarch him to the cruiser. The old officer stood by watching.

And then the loud bang of a gunshot rang out. The woman had come up behind Carlton and fired a shot into her husband's back that missed Carlton by a hair.

"Get that gun out of that woman's hands!" Carlton yelled to the previously inactive policeman. Fortunately, the woman had exhausted her wrath with that one shot, so she put up no resistance. The viper had only struck once. Otherwise, there might have been three dead men as a result – her husband and two policemen.

Carlton put the badly wounded man in his car and shot out for the hospital. He left the old policeman with the handcuffed wife and called for the county to send a deputy out there to get them.

The man had been shot right through a kidney and would have died had there been a delay in getting him medical attention. When he got well enough, Carlton took a warrant for him to swear out and prosecute his wife, but he refused to do so. This was an outcome Carlton had seen before, except that it was usually the wife on the receiving end of the violence.

Johnny Grimes had a nearly identical experience with Carlton when they were riding together as sheriff's deputies some years earlier. Called to a house where a drunken husband was beating on his wife, they both entered and took the man into custody to haul him off to jail. The wife protested at this point saying that she just wanted them to make him stop hitting her – she didn't want him arrested. They told her it was too late for that and he had to go to jail. The husband then said something to her that really ticked her off – a big mistake on his part.

With an officer holding either arm of her husband, she suddenly whipped out a .22 pistol and, without pausing to aim, slingshot fired a round into her husband's stomach. Johnny lurched for her pistol, got her cuffed, and they took the happy couple out to the car for transportation to a hospital and the jail.

Chap 7 — Off Their Meds

Known as the Georgia Lunatic Asylum when it received its first patient in 1842, Central State Hospital, as it was later renamed, grew to be the world's largest mental institution by the start of WWII. Its 200 buildings could accommodate as many as 13,000 patients, many of whom were committed without any sort of due process. Within the walls of this fearsome place, then state-of-the-art psychiatric procedures like electroshock, insulin shock, and lobotomy were routinely carried out by a staff who had no formal training in psychiatry. Many highly disturbed and hyperactive "patients" who were "treated" at Central State returned home as docile shadows of their former selves. Sure, they weren't a trouble anymore, they were as undemanding as a houseplant. The reputation of the place was so widespread that parents could quell unruly children just by saying, "If you don't be good, I'm going to send you to Milledgeville" where Central State was located. For those hapless children who actually were sent there, they were often kept in steel cages.

Fortunately, those abhorrent conditions were in abeyance by the time Carlton was policing. Reforms had been instituted by Georgia Governor Carl Sanders during his 1963-67 term. Sanders' successor, Lester Maddox, the famous axe-handle wielding Atlanta restaurateur and segregationist, had other fish to fry. Ironically, Maddox treated Georgia African Americans better than any previous Georgia chief executive. Governor Jimmy Carter would continue Sanders' mental health reforms, and Central State was becoming a shadow of its former self both in terms of the treatments employed and the number of patients housed at any given time.

With the advent of anti-psychotic medicines, mental patients could be stabilized during relatively brief in-patient treatments and released back to their families where all would be well so long as they stayed on their meds. If the meds stopped being effective, a patient would go back in for adjustments or substitutions to their drugs until they were once again put on an even keel.[27]

Willis Davis[28] was one such patient. He was in and out of Central State since he was boy. As Willis grew towards adulthood – and "grew" is an understatement for a young man who topped out at 6 feet 4 inches and 300 pounds in his twenties – he became more unstable and violent, especially when he stopped taking his medications.

On a Sunday afternoon, just after Carlton and rookie sheriff's deputy Johnny Grimes were getting back on patrol after lunch, Sheriff Wyatt called them to say there's a situation down in Union Point where they needed some help.[29]

"Y'all go on over there and meet them at City Hall," he instructed. "A guy's locked himself in a house and busted a Union Point officer's arm. Just threw him right out the house and broke it."

"Will do, Sheriff," Carlton replied.

"Then go on out to the house with them to get this fella and bring him in here."

The two deputies made a few turns to head over for the short trip to Union Point and its police station in the city hall. When they walked in the front door, they saw that violence had also been inflicted on the offender's parents, both of whom showed obvious signs of being beaten up. They had no broken bones or other serious injuries – at least not yet.

"What happened?" Carlton asked.

The mother spoke up first.

"Our son Willis is a mental patient down there at Milledgeville where he starts behavin' hisself under the medicine they give 'im. So, then they lets 'im out to go home, and he's okay for a couple days."

The father took over at this point.

"Then, Willis just stops takin' them pills and turns crazy agin." He snapped his fingers. "Just like that. He goes to bed nice and gentle like and wakes up like a wildcat that wants to break everything in the house, including Mother and me. It was a doozy this time around."

"Why cain't they just keep 'im down there?!" she nearly screamed. "He's gonna kill the both of us some day!"

"Could'a been today," the father added.

"It nearly was today," she resumed a bit calmer and then told them, "We're tired of him. If y'all got to kill him, go on ahead and do it."

That stopped the conversation for a few seconds until one of the Union Point officers broke it with, "Ma'am, we'll go on out there and see to him."

Carlton broke in at this point – this challenge was right up his alley.

"That's all right. Me and Johnny'll go out there and get him."

He touched Johnny on the sleeve with the back of his hand.

"C'mon, we got work to do." And they headed back out to their car.

When they got to the address, they found themselves looking up at a great-big, three-story house with a high porch surrounding it. It was a steamy August afternoon and all the double-hung windows were shut tight. The house must have been a furnace. It was those windows that had ticked off Willis in the first place. When home and off his meds, Willis considered that big house to be his personal castle where no one from Central State could get at him and tell him what to do. Those windows were the castle's draw bridges, and, of course they had to be closed.

When his father came home and saw the shut windows and felt the stifling heat inside, he went around opening them up to get some badly-needed air moving through the place. Well, Willis didn't take that well and proceeded to beat up his daddy. When his momma came in, she started in on him about his behavior towards his father, so, quite naturally to him, Willis beat her up, too. The parents fled the scene and called the Union Point police, which resulted in an officer with a broken arm and their boy holed up in the house with his draw bridges pulled back tight.

Carlton and Johnny made the steep climb up the porch. Johnny stood off to one side while Carlton strode up and knocked on the latched screen door behind which was the massive front door.

"Willis!" He called out. "We need to talk to you, Willis. Come open the door."

"You better stop knockin'," came a voice from within.

Carlton ignored the warning.

"Willis, c'mon out here or we'll have to come in to get you."

There was no further word from Willis whose preference for action over talk was communicated by the sudden shock and noise of both doors coming straight down on Carlton as if hinged from the bottom. The actual hinges were ripped out of the jamb in the process.

Across the top of that door, now on top of a horizontal Carlton, came the castle's enraged inhabitant, heading directly for Johnny who was astonished at how quickly and how far south this situation had gone. Fortunately for him, Carlton wasn't injured or out for the count and scrambled from under the door to assist his partner. Their combined weights may have equaled Willis's, plus they had four arms to his two. But, Willis was fighting like a madman, which of course he was, and the two deputies were in for it.

They rolled around on the porch until they finally got their gigantic opponent's head hanging off the porch's high edge. Carlton got one of his hands free and jerked a canister of mace from its holster and set about emptying the can in Willis's face. It didn't faze him.

Fortunately for Greene County's finest, two or three more officers arrived to set the odds about right. They finally got Willis pinned down sufficient to get his hands behind him and soundly secured in cuffs. He immediately called it quits and stopped all further struggle.

It was concluded that the only thing to do was to take Willis down the road to Central State. They loaded this now dormant volcano of a man in the back seat of their county car, and off they went on the hour-long drive down to Milledgeville. Not a word came from Willis's mouth.

They got about halfway there when Johnny told Carlton in a quiet voice, "You know, when we finally got him subdued enough to cuff 'im, we just yanked those things real tight on him. There wasn't time to see if they were too tight. We should loosen 'em up." Carlton burbled some air across his lips and said, "Yeah, okay."

So, Johnny, who was driving, looked in the review mirror at Willis, who still hadn't yet said a word, and told him, "Willis, those cuffs are too tight on you. We're going to pull over up here and loosen 'em up for you so they'll feel a little better."

With mace-induced tears running down his face, Willis glared back at him in the mirror and hissed, "If you know what's good for you, you'll leave these cuffs alone." That settled the matter for sure – no further need for concern over their passenger's comfort. Instead, they now focused on how to get him out of the car and into the custody of the Central State staff without further eruption.

The drop-off at Central State for returning customers such as Willis was at the bottom of a steep depression – a welcome sight to the two policemen. They pulled up to a door, and a small man in a white coat came out to the car and opened the back door.

"Willis, do you know me?" the little man asked.

"Yes, Sir," said Willis.

"Get out of the car, Willis," the man instructed.

Willis got out of the car and awaited further instructions.

"Officer, please remove these handcuffs."

Carlton chuckled and looked at Johnny.

Johnny looked at Carlton and said to the man in the white coat. "Look, we just finished fighting him for an hour." He tossed him the key. "You un-cuff him."

So, the man un-cuffed Willis and told him, "Go get on the scales, Willis, and wait for me." He turned back to Johnny and handed him the cuff key while Willis dutifully headed to be weighed in for admission.

"Thank you, officers." And off he went, trailing Willis Brown, now an obedient puppy, into the bowels of the Central State Hospital.

Billie Jean Winchell[30] had some issues. For whatever reason, she would occasionally get the inspiration to strip off her clothes and go running starko down the street. One of her tactics was to go into the bathroom at Herbert Walker's gas station below City Hall in Union Point, get undressed, then head off at a gallop towards the center of town. It was then local law enforcement's duty to remove this visual threat from those in her path. She'd be arrested, wrapped in the officer's coat or a blanket and taken off to jail to await retrieval by her family. Billie's doctor frequently adjusted her meds, but nothing seemed to shut down her predilection for this socially unacceptable pastime. She became a local celebrity of sorts. "There goes Billie Jean!," people would exclaim, mouths agape, and point towards the uncovered jogger out enjoying the fresh air and sunshine. People passing through town were particularly astonished by her performance.

She'd started this practice while in school and had been sent off to Central State for treatment several times. This would take care of things for a while, and then Billie Jean would be back at it again. This went on for years.

One evening, Carlton came into the station and his officer on duty told him, "Carlton, I got the streaker in a cell back there."

Carlton had arrested her a number of times, often having to disarm Billie Jean of the stick she liked to carry to chasten those about to subdue her. He would wrestle her and drag her over to his car to get her in the back. A crowd would gather, but no one ever stepped up to assist him, not that he needed it. Since she was again their guest for the umpteenth time, he thought he'd step back there for a minute and say hello.

The Chief walked over and opened the door to the cells. Billie Jean sat in one of them, a blanket wrapped around her.

"Well, Billie Jean, I didn't even recognize you with your clothes on," Carlton said smiling at her.

She jumped up, threw back the blanket and responded with a grin, "This is me!"

"Yep. That's you, all right!"

It was time for another trip to Milledgeville to get those meds adjusted yet again.

Chap 8 — Changing Jobs

On January 28, 1974,[31] Union Point Mayor John Ben Stewart appointed Carlton Lewis, who would turn 57 in a couple of months, as the new Chief of Police for Greene County's second largest city. The announcement published in *The Herald-Journal* has a photo of an upright and smiling Mayor and a relaxed and pleased new Chief dressed in a uniform associated with his upgraded rank. Stewart was quoted to be "happy to have a man of Mr. Lewis's integrity and police experience to be in charge of the Union Point Police Department."

His appointment must have been very fulfilling to Carlton. Union Point had been his home for years, and he an Eleanor had lived in the same house for most of their marriage. They raised a son there, and although Tom had just graduated from college and was headed for a prominent career in politics and government, he called them daily and visited often. The Lewises were leaders in their church and knew everybody in town. How could Mayor Stewart not recruit this man for this job, which was equal in importance to the mayor's in this small community.

Carlton had served as a deputy sheriff under L. L. Wyatt for nearly nine years, during most of which he was the senior deputy who more or less ran the department for Wyatt. The Sheriff had turned 69 earlier that same month. His health was failing, and he would die four years after Carlton left his service. While one might suspect that Wyatt had taken a good deal of credit that belonged to Carlton and other deputies, Carlton never expressed anything other than the highest admiration for his boss. He knew that Wyatt would not be in that position much longer, and perhaps Carlton wanted it after the curtain had closed on the Wyatt Era. Or perhaps not. What is clear is that Carlton threw himself into his new job as Police Chief and embarked on thirteen additional years of protecting and serving the citizens of Union Point and Greene County.

Carlton settled into his new role as Chief thinking there would be fewer fights and fewer close calls on his life – after all, the milestone age of 60 was just a few years off. Boy, was he wrong.

While the job did involve a change in scenery in terms of where his base of operations was located, other parameters were not much different. Just like the Sheriff's Office, the Union Point PD would only have two or three police officers at any given time. The two departments would also frequently assist each other when some situation required additional officers.

Johnny Grimes, who had ridden with Carlton not long before leaving the Sheriff's Office to join the Georgia State Patrol, recalls that law enforcement was quite a bit different back then from what it is now. You were pretty much on your own as an officer in the field. Backups were few and far between. Greene County only had two cars to transport its three deputies in service to some 11,000 citizens distributed over the county's 406 square miles. Sheriff Wyatt advised his deputies that any time they aren't sleeping, they need to be out patrolling. A 40-hour week and overtime pay were just wishful thinking. The salary was enough to make ends meet – barely. There was little or no training for a new officer other than riding around for a while with a more senior deputy. When he came on in 1972 after four years as an Air Force MP, Grimes was the first Greene County officer to go through mandated training for new police officers held at the University of Georgia campus in Athens. Change was coming from over the horizon, but it would take another couple of decades to settle in.

It was a rough and tumble world, and if you were a deputy that nearly half-a-century ago, you were basically on your own. If you called for backup, it probably had to come from another county if they had an officer available from their handful. That improbable response also required that your radio worked, which depended on the relevant talent being available at the filling station/garage down the street. SWAT teams then existed only in major metropolitan police departments. So, you were pretty much a one-man show dependent mainly on your courage, fighting ability, and intuition rather than formal training.

The contrast with today is remarkable. The estimated Greene County population in 2016 was 17,000, a 55% increase over that of 1960. A 1998 photo shows 31 uniformed officers while the Greene Sheriff's Office presently has 12 officers of rank sergeant or above, six of whom are detectives. Those numbers are aside from the patrol officers each of whom completed a required 408-hour, eleven-week Basic Mandate Law Enforcement program at the Georgia Public Safety Training Center in Forsyth.

The old-school, one-man army approach appealed to men like Carlton Lewis, who likely would have had a hard time in today's policing world. In his retrospective interview, Carlton said that one man then did the work of ten men today. Sounds not far off the mark. One wonders if Carlton, who believed a good policeman was born and not made, would have put up with those 11 weeks of training. It is more likely he would have retired as an executive with the Standard Coffee Company, wealthier but not nearly so satisfied as he was being a peace officer.

L. L. Wyatt died on Good Friday, April 8, 1977, of a sudden catastrophic heart attack. He was 73 years old. Wyatt had served Greene County in law enforcement for 52 years, 37 of which had been as the county's elected sheriff. His sudden death stunned all those in Greene and reached throughout the State of Georgia and even nationally as a result of his fame and longevity as a sheriff. Wyatt's passing spawned a crisis as to who would succeed him.

To many, the answer was Carlton Lewis. The Chief of Police of the City of Union Point had served under Wyatt as chief deputy for nine years before moving to Union Point. Next to Wyatt, there was no one with Carlton's reputation as an effective police officer and honorable man to take on the now-vacated position of Greene County Sheriff. This respect for Carlton was held by the black as well as the white citizens of Greene, and some of the black ministers and leaders came to Carlton urging him to run for the office. His initial response was that he was really getting too old for such a responsible position.

One who did not hesitate to jump into the vacuum was Reese Smith, Wyatt's deputy, who with only a modest education was a man of considerable character. Carlton had trained Reese as a new deputy, and so he knew Reese well and respected him. They had once been in a terrible car wreck together when they were hit by someone who had missed a stop sign. When Carlton came to, he thought Reese was dead and managed to get a radio call in for help before he passed out again. Fortunately, both recovered fully.

Smith's candidacy enhanced the goal of some to get Carlton on the ballot, and many started coming by the Lewis home to twist his arm. Among those was *The Herald-Journal* editor Carey Williams who brought by Bill Kimbrough, then an elected member of the Georgia Public Service Commission, to urge Carlton to run.

Williams remembers pulling up into Carlton's back yard one morning and knocking on the door, which Carlton soon opened.

"What in the world you want here, Carey," Carlton asked, knowing the answer.

"I've got Mr. Kimbrough here, and we want you to run for sheriff," thus wasting no time in confirming Carlton's intuition.

Carlton invited them in and they talked a good while. Kimbrough assured him it wouldn't cost him a dime to run. But, Carlton stuck with his "getting too old for the job" argument while also expressing his concern that the county commissioners would never adequately fund the Sheriff's Office to permit a proper number of deputies. Williams and Kimbrough couldn't disagree with that assessment. They also knew that the Sheriff's salary was not commensurate with the responsibilities and stress of the job.

Wyatt had operated under a legislated "fee system" in which Georgia sheriffs' salaries and operating budgets were derived solely from fines and other fees brought in by their office. Sheriffs kept one-third of those fees from which they paid themselves and their deputies, jailers, and all other staff. The costs for housing and feeding prisoners, purchasing cars, equipment, supplies, maintenance and repairs, i.e. all expenses involved in operating a sheriff's department, came entirely from fees.

Johnny Grimes recalled that when he first signed on with Greene County, people would be lined up from the new jail to the old jail, where they once had the gallows, waiting to pay their fees from traffic violations. The Sheriff's Office would be accommodating to those short on funds by accepting items in kind, like spare tires and tool boxes, that had some value. That's the kind of latitude that was fair play under the fee system.

The Georgia General Assembly eventually repealed the fee system law, but Wyatt had enjoyed this enormous perquisite until four years before his death. His family then found an unexpected fortune in cash in the safe of a bank of which he was a director.[32] The money had been put in a personal non-interest-bearing account. Wyatt's successor would take over without such a fee system and with meager salary support for himself and his small staff, factors not unknown to Carlton Lewis.

It is likely that in his heart Carlton wanted the job, of which he was confident of winning in an election, while his head, his wife, and his physicians argued otherwise. Eleanor had no desire whatever to live in the sheriff's residence at the jail where the sheriff's wife had traditionally been involved in preparing food for prisoners and collecting fees and fines. She just could not see herself living in that awful place. In the end, head won over heart, and Carlton wrote a letter explaining his decision that was published in *The Herald-Journal*. The letter reads:

> I, Carlton Lewis, along with all other Greene
> Countians was greatly saddened when I learned of the
> death of our Sheriff, L. L. Wyatt. Sheriff Wyatt had
> served as a distinguished police officer in our county for
> 52 years. During this time, he gained the admiration and
> respect of all those who knew him, and I am grateful for
> the opportunity I had in working directly under Sheriff
> Wyatt as a Greene County Police Officer for eight years.
>
> I believe that the Sheriff's Office is one that should
> be filled by an individual who not only knows and
> understands the responsibilities of this office, but who
> also is willing to do his very best to see that the citizens
> of Greene County get the best police protection that is
> possible. Anything less than this would be depriving the
> citizens of our county from something that they deserve
> and have paid for with their tax dollars.
>
> Since Sheriff Wyatt's death, I have been contacted
> by many Greene County citizens, white and black, who
> have encouraged me to run for the office. I must admit
> that this has made me very humble and at the same time
> very honored to know that so many people in Greene
> County have placed that kind of trust and faith in me as
> to consider me for such an important position.
>
> However, in considering running for Sheriff, I must
> at the same time consider the advice of my family and
> doctors. Several months ago, I was advised by my
> doctors that I suffered from a slight heart condition. I
> have been advised by my doctors that the additional
> stress and strain which could at times develop with the
> office of Sheriff would certainly not help my condition,
> and because of this it is the wish of my family that I not
> run for Sheriff. I, too, must admit that this might keep
> me from giving the office the kind of leadership I believe
> the county deserves. Therefore, I am not nor will I be a
> candidate for the Office of Sheriff of Greene County. As
> always, it is my intention to assist the newly elected

Sheriff in every way that I can.

I, again, would like to say that words could never express what it has meant to me to have so many people put their confidence and trust in me.

Sincerely

Carlton Lewis

Reese Smith was elected Sheriff of Greene County. This was a trying time for Georgia sheriffs many of whom were succumbing to offers of large bags of cash, that might equal or exceed their annual salaries, in compensation for turning their heads to the night-time arrivals of aircraft loaded with drugs at remote areas of their counties. Many of these sheriffs would be indicted during the 1983-1991 administration of Governor Joe Frank Harris, for whom Tom Lewis would serve as Chief of Staff.

For two reasons, Reese Smith would not be among those dishonored sheriffs. First, he was a man of integrity who would not collude with drug dealers. And, second, Reese was already dead well before those indictments were handed down. He was found dead of a single gunshot wound in a remote part of Greene County on December 15, 1981. His revolver was on the ground beside him. After an inquest, the coroner's jury ruled his death a suicide by a vote of 3 to 2. *The New York Times* mentioned Sheriff Smith's death in a 1984 story on corruption among Southern sheriffs. It provided a hint at a suicide motive.

> State law also now stipulates that no person can serve as sheriff who has ever been convicted of a felony. A sheriff also must have a high school degree or its equivalent.
>
> In Greene County, Sheriff Reese Smith was so worried he would fail the equivalency exam that he dispatched a deputy to take the test for him. Later, a handwriting analysis turned up the fraud and the deputy confessed. Not long afterward, Sheriff Smith was found with a bullet through his head and his service revolver at

his side – apparently a suicide.[33]

While getting caught cheating on a GED exam is no doubt embarrassing, it seems like too small a matter to push a man to suicide. Many then thought, and maintain to this day, that Reese was murdered and the scene staged as a suicide by drug dealers with whom he refused to cooperate. This thinking was reflected by the vote of the coroner's jury. The Georgia Bureau of investigation concluded that no evidence of foul play had been found but did not explicitly state that Reese's death was a suicide.[34] It may never be known with certainty why Reese Smith died while in office at the age of 49.

While Carlton Lewis did not become Greene's sheriff right after Wyatt's 1977 passing, he continued as Chief of the Union Point Police Department for nearly nine more years.

Chap 9 — Why didn't you kill him?

Union Point, Sunday, October 19, 1975, 10:45 am

It was a quiet Sunday morning with most Union Point folks in church. Eleanor was at the First Baptist Church, but Carlton was on patrol duty that morning. He would go to church the coming Wednesday evening. Chief Lewis was filling in for an absent officer, expecting nothing in particular but alert to anything. Parked off the side and perpendicular to the road, Carlton saw Charlie Monfort drive by. Charlie, a young black man not yet 30, was a city employee on the street crew. That Charlie presently did not have a driver's license was known to Carlton, who pulled out and followed him until they came to a good spot for Carlton to pull him over and discuss the matter with him – a minor police action befitting a peaceful church morning.

As they approached Yearwood's filling station just off the main drag in Union Point, Carlton turned on his lights and Charlie responded by braking and pulling into the station. Charlie got out and stood by the driver's side door. Inside the station, a group of men who had gathered for Sunday morning sociability while avoiding Church turned toward the front to watch Charlie get a ticket.

Carlton pulled beside Charlie's car and spoke to him through his open window. "Charlie, I want to check your license."

Charlie got out of the car with a mumble and squatted down right beside his vehicle, as if checking a tire.

Carlton, who was already writing out the citation, repeated his request. "Charlie, I want to see your license. Come over and get in," he said, gesturing to the passenger side of his cruiser.

Without moving, Charlie responded with another mumble.

Carlton lost his patience, laid the book down, and jumped out of his car.

"Get in this car!" he sharply instructed, taking Charlie by the arm to get him up from the squat.

Charlie came up fast with a big wrench in his free hand, striking Carlton in the head several times, knocking him goofy and astonished, but not unconscious.

With blood running down the side of his head from the scalp wounds, Carlton brought out his revolver to shoot his attacker. Charlie caught him by the arm to try to take the gun away from Carlton; instead the gun fell on the concrete between them. Groggy, and knowing what he had to do, Carlton lunged for the gun, but Charlie again got the jump on him by coming up with a knee in Carlton's face, knocking him backward. The gun was then in Charlie's hands.

Cocking the gun, Charlie put it in Carlton's face. The policeman swatted the arm away, grabbed Charlie, and threw him up beside his patrol car. While this was in progress, Charlie still had the gun. The filling station crowd was gathered at the big window, taking all this in without any attempt to aid their police chief. One of them called the Sheriff's office over in Greensboro.

Disarmed during a simple traffic stop by a man he knew and trusted, Carlton's principal emotions were anger and, in particular, embarrassment about losing control of his sidearm and the situation. He did not know what to do next, but he instinctively ordered Charlie to "Give me my gun!" while grabbing him and fighting for the pistol – blood running down his head, neck, and face. The odds were not good for the policeman who was more concerned about being left standing there watching Charlie drive off with his patrol car and gun than he was with losing his life. The tussle brought the two to the backseat side of the car where Carlton managed to get the door open. They both tumbled onto the seat still struggling.

That this brawl was between a 59-year-old officer and a

powerful man half his age never entered Carlton's calculus, which was driven by his rage, his natural predisposition for a fight, and his urgent wish to get his hands on the shotgun in the front seat. At a deeper level, Carlton believed that Charlie wouldn't shoot him so long as they were fighting face-to-face but feared that such honor would evaporate if he turned his back on Charlie.

Taking a chance, he thought he might get the man's attention on something else, so he told Charlie, "I'll call somebody to come down and help out." Why Carlton was doing this was beyond Charlie, who believed he'd knocked the senses out of the Chief, which, indeed, may have been the case. But, it worked – at least temporarily – and Charlie did nothing until Carlton reached down fumbling for his shotgun, yelling "Get out of that car or I'll kill you!"

Charlie fired while coming out of the car. The shot missed and hit the open car door inches from Carlton. Carlton jabbed under his seat for the shotgun and bore down on Charlie. It kept running through his head that the shotgun was loaded with buck shot. While he was looking Charlie square in the eye something kept telling him *don't do it, don't do it, don't do it. You'll blow his head off.*

Carlton raised the gun a bit above Charlie's head and pulled the trigger. BOOM, the gun responded! The desired effect was not produced. Scared for his life now, Charlie shot a second time, the round again missing its target and shattering the car's windshield.

Resolving not make this mistake again, Carlton directed the barrel at Charlie's chest. "Put that gun on my car or I'm going to kill you!"

That inner voice told Carlton to pull the trigger when Charlie pointed the pistol at him the next time. *Blow him in half*, it advised.

"Lay it here or I'll kill you!" Charlie hesitated but wasn't threatening with the gun.

"This is the last time, lay it on my car!"

As Charlie finally obeyed and Carlton retrieved his pistol, the filling station emptied out and the onlookers were running around like birds. Carlton got Charlie in the cruiser's screened back seat, which was now a cage, and the struggle and close encounter with death were now over. Or, should have been.

With the big knocks on the head and the resulting loss of blood, Carlton's mind was not firing on all cylinders. His training got the best of him, and he decided he should have handcuffed his prisoner before putting him in the car. Completely unnecessarily, Carlton opened the door and issued Charlie an order.

"Stick your hands out here and let me put these cuffs on you."

"No! You ain't going to put no hand cuffs on me!"

Carlton leaned in and grabbed Charlie by the arm, pulling him towards the door.

"If you don't put out your hands, I'm going to knock your teeth out." At this point, the starch went out of Charlie and on went the cuffs. One of the filling station spectators ran up to offer his services to the policeman bleeding from his head as if he'd been scalped at Little Big Horn.

"Let me drive you to City Hall, Carlton," he said.

"I'll drive my own durn self over there!" Carlton snapped back and set about doing just that.

This all transpired in very short order during which that call from the filling station had summoned Sheriff Wyatt and a deputy to Carlton's assistance. They met him at City Hall where Carlton removed Charlie from his car and turned him over to the deputy.

L. L. Wyatt took one look at Carlton, dropping his jaw a bit at the bloody sight of his colleague.

"Come on Carlton, let me carry you to the hospital."

"I don't want to go to no hospital."

"Get in this car. I'm going to take you to the hospital and have your head sewn up."

"Ah, my head's all right."

"Get in this car!" Wyatt ordered, settling the issue.

Off they went to the hospital.

Charlie Monfort was charged with two counts of aggravated assault – one for each shot he fired – driving under the influence, obstructing an officer, and driving with a revoked license. Charlie's blood alcohol percentage was 0.24 compared with Georgia's limit of 0.10. Getting drunk on a beautiful fall Sunday morning came razor close to the murder of a police officer.

Bail was set at $23,000 with charges to be presented to the Greene County Grand Jury during its next convening on the fourth Monday of January 1976. At the trial, which lasted five hours followed by a 25-minute jury deliberation, Charlie was inevitably found guilty – after all, the whole thing had transpired before a filling station full of eye witnesses. A sentence of eight years was handed down, and off went Charlie to prison.[35]

While incarcerated, he reportedly said he would get Carlton once he was out. Word of this got back to Carlton who called his bluff and told his friends to tell Charlie that he was always out patrolling the streets. Any time Charlie wanted to come after him would be just fine.

Charlie would serve half his sentence before being paroled to return to Union Point. The two men would thereafter pass each other on the street without speaking. Charlie never came after Carlton.

During the trial, the judge and the DA had both asked Carlton why he didn't kill Charlie Monfort – he had every justification for doing so.

Carlton Lewis' response was "I don't know. I think the good Lord just told me not to do it."

Losing his gun to Charlie Monfort troubled Carlton enormously. Although it was an obvious matter of self-preservation, the indignity of allowing himself to be disarmed was far more troubling to him. He vowed to never let that happen again, and he asked Eleanor to make him a waist holster for a derringer, his last resort after losing his main weapons.

When Tommy heard about this, he asked his father if it was tight and uncomfortable to wear that gun under his belt. Carlton replied with "Heck no, Tommy. It's a different kind of comfort to have that backup gun there. I'll never be put in a situation again without a gun like I was with Charlie."

"Tell you what Tommy, I'll give you my guns someday after I retire. They'll help you protect yourself and your own family."

Tommy didn't say much in reply. He didn't like thinking about some future when his father was too old to be a policeman.

In January 1977, the House and Senate of the Georgia General Assembly adopted a resolution stating that, "Chief Carlton Lewis is hereby commended for his outstanding and dedicated service as a law enforcement officer in this state." The resolution cited his courage and restraint in overcoming the assault by Charlie Monfort as well as his efforts in resolving the murder of Reuben Flynt. Both had occurred in 1975. A photo in *The Herald-Journal* for February 15, 1977 Governor George Busby presenting the resolution to Carlton. Carlton's son Tom, who would serve as Chief of Staff to Busby's successor, Joe Frank Harris, also appears in the photograph. Governor Harris would later appoint Carlton to serve as one of some twenty individuals on his Criminal Justice Coordinating Council.

Chap 10 — The Peacocks' Call

While Carlton Lewis's 22-yr policing career was punctuated with plenty of action and risks, the great majority of his days commenced and concluded with the routine quietness that ought to surround a thinly-populated, rural Georgia community. Sure, when the situation called for it, Carlton would light up his afterburners and go after his goal with remarkable energy and fierceness. But, he had a softer side, which is what the folks of Union Point virtually always saw in their encounters with "Mr. Carlton."

Carlton felt that "to be a good policeman, you've got to love people," and he demonstrated this love and desire to help the people he protected in various ways. He particularly loved children – most notably, of course, his son – and wanted his community to be a fine place for them to be raised. Here are a few vignettes of Mr. Carlton's humanity.

Union Point, ca. 1968

Joel McCray grew up in Union Point with the Lewises, attended the First Baptist Church with them, loved "Miss Eleanor," and regarded her and Carlton as a comforting part of his everyday life. When he was twelve, Joel bought himself a pair of peacocks that he named Victoria and Alvin. He built a pen for them in his back yard, and the family loved to sit out and watch the beautiful birds strut around the yard and interact with each other. When mating season arrived, the charm was seriously diminished, particularly for the McCray's neighbors, when the birds frequently called out to each other.

Now, the first time you ever hear the call of a peacock, you will be certain that a woman is in serious trouble, and you may reach for your phone to punch 911. The high-pitched voice of this avian beauty is remarkably close to the shrill call for help from a desperate and life-threatened woman. That's bad enough in itself, but the birds would crank up this racket about 3 am and keep it up until daylight. It was this noise that was sufficiently disturbing folks in earshot of Joel's peacocks to result in their complaining to the police.

So, one day when Joel came home from school, Mr. Carlton pulled up by the back yard, rolled down his window and said, "Joey."

"Yes, Sir."

"I think you know why I'm here."

"Yes, Sir," Joey repeated.

"You know, I've arrested a lot of people and taken in a lot of things in my life for breakin' the law and disturbin' the peace, but I've never had to arrest a peacock."

Joey's instinct about why Deputy Lewis was there was thus confirmed.

"What are we going to do, Joey?"

"Don't worry Mr. Carlton, I'll get rid of the them. I have a cousin in the country, and I'll give 'em to him."

Carlton frowned and replied, "Joey, this just breaks my heart to ask you to do that 'cause I know how much you enjoy them. But, after all, we have to consider other people, and I don't want to have to arrest your peacocks."

Joel McCray is today a long-time florist in Greensboro and serves as the Greene County Historian. He fondly remembers "Mr. Carlton" as "always so considerate, giving everyone the benefit of the doubt."

✢ ✢ ✢ ✢

Rhodes Sports Corner and General Store on Sibley Avenue lives up to its name in offering countless items for almost any purpose. If you can't find what you are looking for there, it isn't in Greene County. It is also one of the popular gathering places for the men in the community, a status that was held many years ago by the Sinclair filling station on the corner where the Athens Highway crosses Lamb Avenue.

That station was owned by Carlton Lewis in the 1950s, years before he found his calling in police work. Lanier Rhodes, Union Point's current mayor and owner of the Sports Corner along with his wife Jill, remembers being allowed to sit with the men at Carlton's filling station on evenings after dinner when they would wander down there to smoke, shoot the breeze, and enjoy an hour or so of male sociability before calling it a night. Lanier well remembers those evenings, frequently accompanied by laughter, when "Mr. Carlton's disciples" convened at the Sinclair station.

The guys would drag their chairs outside and line them up in a semi-circle along the station's front wall facing the gas pumps with the chair backs forward. They'd all sit like that with arms draped over the chair backs and Carlton holding court, the smoke from their cigarettes filling the air. They would talk about things that had happened that day and whatever topic was offered up for discussion. Politics, sports, community news and gossip, whatever popped into somebody's head would be brought to the attention of all. The station was situated along the main drag into "downtown" Union Point, a good location for a filling station. The railroad ran just behind it, and the boys would sometimes have to delay their talk a bit as a train clattered by, blowing its whistle on the approach into town. As twilight deepened into darkness, men would one-by-one announce they'd better head on back home to a wife tolerant of this odd male herd behavior.

The Rhodes children, now grown, have their own remembrances of Mr. Carlton, who was their Police Chief by then. Kim Rhodes was an excellent basketball player, and her parents set up a goal for her outside the store so she could practice whenever she liked. When the Chief would come by on rounds and she was outside shooting hoops, he would stop for a while and sit on a low wall outside their store to watch Kim hone her skill. She recalls how comforting it was to have him there. He wouldn't play ball with her; he'd just watch for a while and praise her. Having him there made her want to do her best for him. When it was time for Carlton to move on, he would give her a piece of bubble gum and some parting praise.

When Kim's little brother Trey was three years old, Carlton would stop by the Rhodes house and ask if he could take Trey for a ride in his police car. The Rhodes would invariably say 'sure,' and off would go Trey and Mr. Carlton for a ride around town and a stop at the drug store where Carlton would buy Trey a coke and have him read the newspaper out loud. Trey would years later represent his home area in the Georgia House of Representatives.

Sometimes, the peace and quiet of Union Point could get boring to a police chief who loved the action when it came to him or when he went looking for it. On one occasion, Carlton had the opportunity to get to know a famous singer and actor and participate in filming a movie. What could be more exciting?

His office phone in Atlanta rang, and Tom Lewis picked it up.

"You want to meet Kenny Rogers?" his Dad asked.

"What are you talking about, Dad?

"I got Kenny Rogers in town. They're here makin' a movie."

This was in 1981, and Tommy was now married and working in Atlanta. He and his wife Patty drove down to Union Point to meet the famous Country Music Hall of Famer who had come to Georgia to film the made-for-TV movie *The Coward of the County*. The movie dramatized Rogers' hit song of the same name, and most who saw it liked it.

Kenny had a trailer set up at the film site to which he would retire between shooting calls. So, Carlton took his son and daughter-in-law to see the star in his trailer where they chatted for some time. Carlton had come on board after getting a call asking him for a recommendation for a security person for the film star while there on location. Thinking, what the heck, he'd do it himself, he was soon signed up for the duration of the shoot.

He later told Tommy, "You know, son, that's the most boring stuff I've ever seen. I wish I'd never signed up on this thing." Tom laughed and Carlton continued. "They spent the whole dad-gum day going back and forth in the gym over there and got no more than twenty seconds of the movie done that whole time. I got myself into the wrong thing on this deal. I'll sure be glad when it's done!"

One day when the shooting was on hold, Kenny came up to Carlton and said, "Chief, I want to go fishin'. You got any good spots around here?"

Carlton said, "I'll take you myself." So, Kenny, his wife Marianne, and Carlton headed off for an afternoon of drowning worms at the "old railroad pond."

Kenny Rogers was a fine man, but Carlton resolved to never repeat the mistake of providing security during filming. It was too much like watching grass grow.

Ask most any wife, and she'll tell you that there's a boy inside her man that is always on the lookout for adventure with a willingness to break the rules to get it.

Case in point – another time Tom's phone in Atlanta rang. It was Carlton checking in with his son.

"Hey, Dad, how you doin'?" Tom greeted his father.

"Well, Tommy, I'm fine now that I'm back from having Doc Billy sew up my durn finger."

"What'd you do to your finger, Dad."

"Well, I was walking home for lunch and there was a train that was blocking the crossing. Now, I've never done this before, and I know I shouldn't have done it this time, but I got the notion that instead of walking around or through the train, I'd just cross over the top."

"Are you kidding me, Dad?! You're the police Chief. You can't do that?"

"Well, maybe you're right. But you know how these ideas get in your head and sound solid as rock, at least at the time. Besides, I thought it'd be fun!"

"Yeeaah, well, I guess," Tom replied skeptically.

"Good. I thought you'd agree. So, I walked up to a car where there was this ladder up the side and was on top of that thing in no time at all. Nice view from there when you look up and down the train."

"I'm sure there was, Daddy. So, how'd you cut your finger so bad you had to get stitches?"

"I was just up there a minute, you know, and I didn't want to take too much time for lunch, so I climbed down the ladder on the other side. Would have been no problem at all if the dad-burn train hadn't started to move."

"Move!" was all Tommy could blurt out.

"It sure did and with a lurch that knocked me loose from the ladder. When that happened, I naturally tried to grab a rung, but my ring got caught on it and ripped up a big chunk of skin on that finger."

"Ouch!" Tommy interjected.

"So, I went to the drug store to get sumthin' to patch me up. They said it's a bad cut, and I'd best go to the doctor to get it fixed."

"Man, you were lucky it didn't rip your whole finger off."

"I suppose so. Anyway, I went on over to Billy's – lunch would have to wait a bit – to have him look at it. When he mopped the blood away, he frowned and said, *I'm gonna have to stitch you up,*

Carlton, but first I got to cut that ring off to get at that skin flap.' So, I told Billy, *'No you ain't gonna cut that ring off'* He looked at me and said, *'And why won't I cut that off?'* So, then I said, *'Look, Doc. I'm married to a red-headed woman, and if you cut that ring off I'm goin' to have more explainin' to do than all the trouble this finger would ever cause me.'"*

Dr. William Rhodes now fully understood Carlton's reluctance to lose that ring at the risk of losing his finger. He went to work on the finger and managed to nudge the skin back underneath the ring for stitching, knowing for certain that Eleanor wouldn't have hesitated to have him cut the ring had she been there with her husband.

The Lewises regularly attended the Union Point Baptist Church, which had been organized in 1872. Carlton was a deacon and served on many committees, including the re-building committee when the church burned in the early 1950s.[36] He also sang in the choir. He always positioned himself in a back corner, closest to the door, so that when his professional services were required he could discretely remove himself with minimal fuss and distraction to his singing partners. Tom remembers on several occasions being in church listening to and watching the choir and then turning his attention back to the preacher. And, when it was the choir's time to perform again, his father would be gone. Sometimes Carlton would just as magically reappear later in the service, which, this being a Baptist church, might take a while. Other times, his dad might be gone all afternoon. In any event, Tom and his mom would hear about it at dinner.

One of their favorite pastors was the Reverend Charles Kopp, who was noted for his eloquent prayers during church services, funerals, and at other events he officiated or gave the blessing.

Eleanor remarked at lunch after church one Sunday that she just loved to hear their pastor pray.

Carlton, famous for his one-liners, responded to Eleanor's admiration for Reverend Kopp's bowed articulation by saying, "He's the only man I know that when he prays, he has to stop and explain to God what he's sayin'." In a chance meeting of Tom Lewis and the author with Pastor Kopp's son David, a Greensboro attorney, he responded when he heard this story, "Can you imagine eating lunch at home when those kinds of prayers got started? You'd about starve before they got over with!"

Mary and Harold Finch are long-time residents of Union Point who are the few still living who remember Carlton and Eleanor as friends. Mary was the assistant to the president of Farmer's Bank, and Harold worked at the Union Manufacturing sock mill where he rose to a supervisory position. They attended the First Baptist Church with the Lewises and enjoyed their company inside and outside of church.

Mary remembers that Carton loved people, and the more people he could communicate that to, the better he liked it. He particularly relished getting together with the Finches and others from the ladies Sunday school class who would invite their husbands for an evening of good food and socializing. That often entailed a drive in the church bus up the road to Athens, the University of Georgia's hometown, which boasted far more good eating establishments than did Union Point. Mary recalled that "Carlton loved to eat, but he loved to be with friends even more." These outings went on from the time when Carlton was in the dry-cleaning business and continued after he was chief of police in the Finch and Lewis home town.

In those later years, she knew that those who worked for Carlton really liked him and often thinks of Carlton having told her that "if you want people to respect you, you've got to show them respect." That theme recurs in Carlton's interaction with friends and acquaintances as well as with those for whom circumstances required their being dragged kicking and screaming, biting and cussing into the back seat of his patrol car. Such tussling was a short-term necessity after which the respect would be shown in their fair treatment.

Carlton and Eleanor together had a modest but adequate income to provide for a comfortable living without a lot left over. And yet they made room for charity to others in their tight budget. In addition to routine donations to their church, which they considered as much of part of the cost of living as was their grocery bill, they routinely gave money, food, and clothing to a black woman with no husband to support her several children. Her name was Clarice, and on many occasions when circumstances closed in on her financially, she would knock on the Lewis's door and ask if they might help her. They always did. Other times, Carlton would hear that Clarice needed some help and he would get word to her to send one of her boys around. He would then send the child home with a twenty-dollar bill for his mother. This went on for years.

Another side of Carlton was his blithe willingness to ignore acceptable behavior for a policeman under certain circumstances. Here is an example.

Carlton was always on the alert for anything or anyone coming in to his community that might adversely affect his people. Occasionally, as in the following example, he might have stepped on the Constitution just a little bit. But, one suspects that Union Point residents would have admired him all the more if they knew the intensity of his vigilance on their behalf.

Tom and Carlton were walking to Miz Huff's, where Carlton ate lunch several times a week, when a slow-driving, out-of-state car glided by them. Carlton eyed it intently.

"'Scuse me a second," he told Tom.

Carlton whistled at the driver and instructed him to pull over.

"What in the world is he doing," Tom thought and watched his father sidle up to the driver's side window.

"Where you from?" he asked in a great economy of words.

"Uh, Connecticut," was the wary reply.

"Who you visitin'?" came next.

The man named a Union Point resident.

"How long you going to be here?" The third degree continued while Tom's astonishment heightened. The man told him.

"We have a peaceful little community, and I hope you have a good visit here. I guess you'll be gone about next Tuesday. Right." It was a statement, not a question.

"Yes, Sir," the Yankee replied nervously.

"Okay, then. All right – just wanted to know." Carlton's nod told the man he could move on, which he did at a snail's pace no doubt wondering what planet he'd landed on.

"Uh, Dad, I don't think you can do that. Can you?" a shocked son asked his father.

"Sure you can. Let's go eat."

October 2017, in the mountains near Waynesville, North Carolina

The Tom and Patty Lewis clan was gathered near Asheville at their mountain cabin for a fall weekend. Their supper of pecan-crusted trout, fresh caught that morning by Tom and son Wes, was finished with the dishes stacked in the sink for later. Now it was time to sit on the front porch and watch the sun set from their high-elevation perch. It was going to be a good one as there was just the right mix of distant clouds with clear blue to promise a memorable show as the sun dipped below the horizon.

It was time to reminisce, and, as it so often did, the conversation drifted to memories of Carlton, a larger-than-life figure to his grandchildren. It was just the five of them as Wes's and Ellen's spouses had taken their own children for a walk down the dirt road.

Wes was six when Carlton died and had his own memories of Paw Paw. Two years younger than Wes, Ellen's recollections of her grandfather were mostly colored by sessions like this evening's. Tom's and Patty's youngest daughter Shannon's image of her father's father, who she never met, was entirely based on all she had heard about him and his adventures over the years.

After a good laugh at Carlton's audacity in pulling over the Connecticut visitor to probe his reasons for being in Union Point, Wes introduced the next story.

"And, then there was that time I helped him arrest that drunk driver?" he brought up with a grin.

Tom laughed and all eyes turned to Patty, who frowned and shook her head slowly before breaking into a smile as the memory of that episode returned....

#

Carlton slapped his knee and said, "I got to go back to City Hall right quick to pick up somethin' I forgot to bring home with me."

He reached down and picked up Wes, a curious little boy just short of his fourth birthday. Tom and Patty were spending the day with his parents before heading back to Cartersville after supper. Wes and his two-year-old sister Ellen were there to visit their Paw Paw and Maw Maw, who were thrilled to have them.

"Y'all don't mind my grandson riding down there with me, do you?"

The anxious parents looked at each other before Patty said, "You won't be gone long, will you?"

"No, we'll just run down there and come right back. No more than ten minutes."

"Alright, then," Patty replied a bit nervously.

"Come on, Wes, you and me are goin' for a little ride in a police car." He exaggerated "police" with a long "o."

Wes had no problem with that at all.

Carlton headed down North Rhodes Street to take the railroad crossing to Lamb Avenue and then the back way into his departmental office at City Hall on Veazey.

As he approached Hart, a car pulled out up ahead of him and also proceeded down Rhodes. The man should have waited until Carlton passed the intersection before pulling out, but he would let that one slide. What he couldn't abide was the man's weaving down Rhodes.

Carlton looked over at Wes and said, "Well, grandson, it looks like we may be a little delayed from what I told your mother. You don't mind though, do ya?"

Wes looked up at him as if to say, "Nope, fine with me."

So, Carlton turned on his lights and burped the siren. Wes loved that noise. The weaver's tail lights came on, and he slowed to a stop smack in the middle of Rhodes.

Carlton opened his car door and reached over to pick up Wes. "You're goin' with me, young man. You'll like this!" He didn't want to leave the boy alone in a car that had a shotgun under the front seat.

With his left arm wrapped around Wes, Carlton walked up and knocked on the driver's window, which dutifully rolled down. The man's focus was barely, but sufficiently, clear to see the novelty of a policeman about to arrest him while holding a little boy.

"What'd he do wrong, Sheriff? Drive without a license?" The man was pleased with his own cleverness.

Carlton wasn't.

"I'm the Police Chief, not the Sheriff. And you're under arrest for drunk driving. Get out of the car."

Wes grinned down at the fellow, who returned it in kind as he got to his feet. Carlton led his wobbly captive back to the police cruiser and opened the back door.

"Get on back there, Pardner, and I'll take you jail to sober up. They'll give you a bite to eat and lots of water to wash the booze out of you. First, we got to drop my little grandson off, or his momma will call the police on me."

The man awkwardly got in the back seat, cramped to very little leg room by the partition between it and the front. He remained cheerful throughout.

On the way back to Paw Paw's house, Wes and the prisoner talked to each other as the young boy stood facing back from the front seat, both hands propped against the partition. As he approached the house, Carlton saw Eleanor, Patty, and Tom standing out front. They were clearly anxious over the delay. He knew the anxiety would swing in a not-good direction when they heard the reason for that delay. "Oh, well, I'll just have to take my medicine," he thought.

After the appropriate dose was administered, Carlton returned to his car and backed out to head to the jail, Wes watched it all bugged eyed, held up his hand, and loudly said, "Bye, Bye!"

The man smiled a big one, waved, and said "Bye, Bye!"

The next morning, Carlton let him go.

Chap 11 — Politics

Politics – there's no avoiding it. Especially if you are the police chief. There's an old saying in universities that the fights among academics are so bitter because the stakes are so small. The same might be said about the leadership of small towns. But, when you think about it, the election of a mayor is as important to the residents of Union Point as it is to the citizens of Atlanta.

The Police Chief of Union Point, Georgia, is an appointee of the town's City Council, which effectively means the Chief is beholden to the mayor for his job. So, if you are the Chief and like your job, you had better get along with the Mayor. Things were fine when John B. Stewart was mayor and made Carlton the Chief. Stewart had been in the dry-cleaning business with Carlton and was the best man at his wedding. They went way back and saw eye-to-eye.

The same could not be said of Stewart's successor, Scotty Scott. Sometimes, big problems have small triggers. In this case it was sausage biscuits. Scott had been on the City Council and served as Mayor *pro tempore* for years before he was elected mayor himself. Carlton thought he would be a good mayor, but the relationship soured and Scott gave him the fits at every turn. It was the classic case of attempting to micro-manage an agency in the charge of someone down the chain of command. Carlton referred to this as "nit-picking," and it was annoying the heck out of him.

"Carlton, why don't you do this. Why don't you do that," he complained about the Mayor. He told his boss and the rest of the City Council, "When y'all hired me, you did it to put me in charge of the police force. That's my job. You don't know how to police. If I'm not doing a good job, then fire me. That's your job. But don't mess with the police force – I'm its chief! You make the laws and I'll see that they're enforced, but don't be trying to run the police department."

Things were better for a while – until the Mayor homed in on Carlton's practice of having a morning sausage biscuit in his office. "Carlton, don't you think you shouldn't be eating one of those biscuits every morning in here," the Mayor advised one morning when he dropped by. Well, that was it. Carlton was done with this guy. The town needed a new mayor, and Carlton knew who it needed to be.

Former Mayor Stewart had a son – Ben, Jr. He had political ambitions but was more cerebral and didn't have the force of personality of his father. No matter how smart and sincere you are as a candidate, a shallow but glad-handing back-slapper can run over you at the polls. That had happened to Ben when he ran for the city council.

Carlton went to Ben Stewart and encouraged him to run and pledged to help him take the job away from Scotty Scott. Ben got on the ballot. Carlton knew that if you are a political appointee in a small town and decide to get active politically, you had better have eyes in the back of your head and be subtle at every step you take. If you go out and overtly campaign for an opponent to your boss, you had better update your resume because you will soon be needing it.

Everybody in Union Point was accustomed to Carlton's long walks, especially the business people in town. He would drop by their places to ask if all was okay and to chat for a few minutes before engaging those at the next business along his path. Inevitably, the mayor's race would come up in these conversations, and Carlton would casually put in a plug for Ben.

"You know that Ben Stewart, he's a smart fellow. I am telling you the truth. He's really got lots of abilities, and he would make a really good Mayor," he would tell folks. "And, Ben's got plenty of experience from watching his daddy over the years. I know he ain't friendly, but who cares about that? We want to elect a good mayor to improve the town. Now, there's nothin' bad about the one we got now, but this man here, I honestly believe he'd make us a fine mayor."

When Scott was defeated, he came to Carlton befuddled by his loss. "Carlton, what happened?" he asked and then went on, "There was more organization and more planned professional work that went on here than I've ever seen in my life."

"Well, I don't know about that, Mayor, but you may be right."

Ben Stewart served as Mayor for 25 years following his defeat of Scotty Scott in 1979 and was credited with revitalizing the downtown area of Union Point. He also owned much of Union Point. But, his Stewart Finance business was alleged to have charged exorbitant interest rates, approaching 100%, on loans to poor people. In May 2003, the Securities and Exchange Commission filed complaint[37] in the U.S. District Court against Stewart in connection with multiple illegalities that scooped up some millions of dollars in loans and investments in a pyramid scheme that supported the Mayor's lavish lifestyle. Ben Stewart committed suicide the following May, just hours after learning of his impending indictment for fraud.[38] The magnitude of all this went far beyond the small town of Union Point as there were sixty Stewart Finance offices throughout five states. The tragedy emanating from the little town of Union Point attracted national attention.[39]

As often happens following political battles, one-time opponents become close friends down the line. Such was the case with Scotty Scott and Carlton Lewis. Scotty would be one of the main speakers at Carlton's 1986 retirement dinner. One wonders if sausage biscuits ever came up for discussion.

If you want to win an election in a 50-50 county, you have to motivate and get out the black vote. This process depended upon having positive and trusting relationships with black leadership, which tended to devolve to the ministers of the African-American congregations. As a policeman who had arrested and jailed more blacks than whites, often through rough physical encounters, Carlton's relationship with black ministers was symptomatic of how they viewed his fairness toward their community. The outcomes for blacks he'd taken to jail was generally appropriate to their offenses. So, they would always listen to him and agree to host him and others from the county leadership in their churches to promote candidates and seek their congregations' support. Then on election day, you encourage them to organize voter transportation to the polls and provide gas money for those taking them there.

Tom Lewis vividly remembers when, as a college student, he was working for the election of David Gambrell to the US Senate. Governor Jimmy Carter had appointed Gambrell to fill out the term of Richard Russell when Russell died in 1971. The following year, Gambrell lost the Democratic primary to Sam Nunn, who would be Georgia's senator for 25 years. Russell never had opposition, so when his era ended some 15 aspiring democrats jumped into the fray. Thus, Gambrell had serious opposition not only from Nunn, but from former Governor Ernest Vandiver, the Reverend Hosea Williams, and one J. B. Stoner who was a remarkably overt segregationist who once said that Adolf Hitler had been too moderate. Stoner would be indicted five years later for the 1958 bombing of Birmingham's Bethel Baptist Church.[40]

Although Gambrell lost the election, he carried Greene County. Tom attributes that entirely to his father's access to the black churches so that Tom could meet with the ministers and talk to the church members. Carlton always went with him. Gambrell won Greene handily, taking 48% of the vote. Vandiver came in second at 27% with Nunn as a distant third at 9%. Polar opposites if ever there were such, Stoner and Williams tied with 5%.

It was Gambrell's only victory in a 20-county region in that part of the state and among his largest statewide.[41]

On one occasion, Carlton got involved in county politics in a slightly unorthodox fashion. This was in 1982, and Joe Frank Harris was running for governor with stiff opposition in the primary runoff from Congressman Bo Ginn. Tom, who was organizing and helping in running the Harris campaign, got a report that someone was going around taking up *Harris for Governor* signs out in Greene and surrounding counties and putting up Ginn signs in their place. So, Tom called up his dad and apprised him of the situation.

"Well, I'll get to the bottom of this," his father responded sharply.

"Uh, Dad, this happens all the time, and maybe a police chief ought not to take it too seriously and do something inappropriate," Tom cautioned him.

"I'll report back," Carlton replied while hanging up.

Tom thought, "Uh oh."

Carlton called Tom the next day.

"You're not going to have any more problem with signs down here," he reported.

"Dad, what did you do?" Tom asked warily.

"We found out who's been doin' it. He won't do it anymore."

Tom guessed all his father had to do was to ask around until somebody told on the culprit. Then, Carlton must have gone and had a little chat with him. Tom didn't want to know the specifics of that conversation.

Harris beat Ginn by 10 percentage points in the primary and went on to win the general election in a landslide.[42] Tom went with Governor Harris to the Georgia Capitol and two years later was promoted to Chief of Staff.

Chap 12 — A Late-Night Phone Call

Union Point City Hall, May 16, 1979, half past midnight

There's nothing that brings dread to a police chief's heart like the ringing of his telephone long after he's gone to bed. The call this night was to be the worst in Carlton Lewis's life.

Union Point police officers Michael Cook and Thomas Rowry were patrolling on a quiet and uneventful Wednesday night just after midnight. Both men were junior officers in their twenties, and the only slightly remarkable thing about them was that Tommy was black while Mike was white. It was likely to be one of those boring nights when coffee was badly needed to fight off boredom's drowsiness. They were discussing heading back to City Hall for a cup of Joe when they saw that the car approaching them was weaving and wandering off and on the road's shoulder. They drove past the car without the driver seeming to notice them. It was clear that this guy needed pulling over, so they did a U-turn to follow him for another block before turning on their lights.

The driver, who was black, pulled over without much hesitation and both officers exited their car to take a good look at the guy. The cop wariness in these situations had eliminated the need for caffeine, and Cook and Rowry were alert to any bad signs that the man might exhibit. In a situation like this, it was their habit that Rowry would talk to the detainee if he or she was black and vice versa for Cook. So, Tommy approached the driver's side door while the window was being rolled down. The smell of alcohol wafted Tommy's way. Yet another drunk driver. This one's license identified him as Robert

Lewis Wallace with a Wilkes County address.

Wallace was agreeable to stepping out of the car for the classic sobriety field test of walking a straight line. He failed.

"Mr. Wallace, you appear to be intoxicated, and we're going to take you back to the station for a breathalyzer test. Do you understand that?" Tommy Rowry asked the man.

"Course I do," Wallace replied holding out his hands to be cuffed.

"No need for that, it's just a short ways over there," Mike Cook informed him after judging their prisoner to be a harmless drunk. Mike took the wheel while Tommy sat in back with Wallace to ask a few questions.

"What were you doing out so late driving in your condition?" Tommy asked.

"Well, see, I'd been at Teresa's – she's my girlfriend – and we were having a few. She started in on me about gettin' a job, so I decided to show her and told her then and there I was leavin' for Atlanta to find work in the mornin'."

"Not the best decision, huh, Mr. Wallace." Tommy observed to him.

"Seein' as where I'm sittin', I reckon not."

That exchange pretty much filled up the drive time to City Hall where they led their detainee to the front counter. The breathalyzer was brought out and soon registered a blood alcohol level of 0.11, not the worst they'd seen but adequate for a DUI charge.

Tommy delivered Wallace the news.

"In accordance with State Law, you are legally intoxicated. What happens next is that we lock you up for four hours to sober up, after which you can be released on bond. You understand?"

"You gonna lock me up? For four hours?" The man was oddly crestfallen at the prospect.

"Yessir, that's standard procedure. Just stay put here a couple of minutes while I go get a cell ready for you. That four hours will pass in no time."

That didn't cheer up the now depressed prisoner who stood alone at the counter with Mike Cook. Wallace turned to Cook.

"Please, Sir, please, I can't take being locked up. Can't I just sit out here and sober up? I won't make no trouble, I promise! Please!"

Mike had a touch of sympathy for the pathetic man, but he had to tell him, "No, I'm sorry, but procedure requires us to put you in a cell for a few hours like Tommy explained. You'll be fine. We'll get you some coffee and a peanut butter sandwich to help get you sober and on your way."

This should have helped, but it didn't. Wallace looked like he might break out in tears. Mike thought to himself *let's get this over with* and took Wallace by the arm to lead him to the cell. "C'mon, Robert."

As if struck by lightning, Wallace galvanized into a madman, grabbing Mike by the arm and yanking the .357 magnum from Mike's holster. Mike, who was no match physically for the much larger Wallace, tried to retrieve his weapon. Tommy heard yells from the scuffle and ran to assist Mike just as the .357 roared, delivering a round to Mike's stomach. As Mike hit the floor, Tommy saw the muzzle flash and felt a sting high in his body. He turned to flee, and Wallace fired at him again. Missing Tommy, Wallace redirected his attention back to Mike, stooping to shoot him in the head from less than two feet away. Miraculously, Mike jerked his head to the side as the gun thundered for the fourth time, the slug slamming into the floor. The powder burns on his face were nothing compared to the gunshot wound in the abdomen.

Wallace bolted out of city hall and fled in the police car that had brought him there. Mike managed to call for help before passing out, not knowing where Tommy had gone.

Carlton put the phone back on the cradle, squeezed his eyes tight for a second. Adrenalin coursed through his system.

Eleanor stirred next to him. "What is it? Is it bad?"

"Don't know yet. I gotta' go. Go back to sleep, Hon," he replied in as calm a voice as he could muster, focusing now on putting his clothes on and getting to City Hall.

He made the trip in about two minutes, but when he got there Mike Cook was already in transit. He had many weeks of hospitalization ahead of him, but he would survive.

Tommy Rowry was missing. Approaching sirens were beginning to disturb the peace of the night as Carlton went looking for Tommy. If Tommy had been shot, he might be laying somewhere nearby seriously wounded. Carlton didn't have far to look.

A trail of blood thinned out, pointing down Scott Street. And, there at Herbert Walker's filling station on the corner next to City Hall, Carlton saw a body under the station's pump shed. *That must be Tommy.*

It was Tommy – Officer Thomas Rowry, Jr., age 27, married three years to Doris, father of their little boy Thomas Rowry, III – dead from massive loss of blood as a result of the gunshot wound to his throat. Murdered by a drunk driver gone berserk at the prospect of spending a few hours sobering up in a cell.

"Yes, Hon, it's bad, very bad," Carlton mumbled to himself.

The corner of Scott Street and Lamb Avenue in Union Point was soon lined with Greene County and Georgia State Patrol cars, their flashing lights ripping up the night. Wilkes County officers were racing towards the address Tommy and Mike had recorded for Robert Lee Wallace. The GBI would be on the crime scene in forty minutes.

The manhunt was underway.

Wallace did indeed hightail it back to Wilkes, but he went to his brother's home instead of his own. He told his brother about the shooting and learned that one of the officers was dead. It was time to get some more distance from there, and Wallace decided to get lost in the big city. So, off to Atlanta he went. Wilkes County is northeast of Greene, so he skirted that county on the north side towards Athens and then west to Atlanta. His brother had loaned him his car and given him a .22 caliber magnum pistol in addition to the shotgun Wallace had taken from the patrol car before ditching the vehicle in the woods not far from his brother's place.

Once in Atlanta, he ended up hiding in the basement of a dark and apparently vacant building on Gilbert Street. He was wrong about that, and the noise he made just before 4 am woke up the woman upstairs who immediately called the police. When the barricaded basement door was busted in, Atlanta PD officers arrested him without any resistance. Wallace's main concern was for the shortbread cookies he had dropped and scattered on the floor. Then the officers found the two guns. Alerted to the Union Point shooting, the police asked Wallace if he'd been involved in that. He readily confessed saying he'd shot one of the officers but couldn't remember about the second one.[43]

"Why'd you shoot him?" an officer asked.

"Well, they was just too easy goin' about everything and weren't payin' attention to what they was doin'. So, I grabbed one guy's gun and shot him."

"They weren't abusing you in any way?"

"Nope. They'd been real nice to me. They just shoulda payed more attention to things."

Wallace told them he considered pulling a gun on them and having them shoot him. When asked about it later, one of the officers, a woman, told a reporter, "If we had known he was the perpetrator, we probably would have shot him." Her fellow officer pretty much said the same thing.[44]

✛ ✛ ✛ ✛

Wallace was indicted for murder and other charges in Greene County on July 23, 1979 with the trial scheduled for the 26th. That date was further postponed until September after Wallace hired an Atlanta lawyer named Ed Augustine who then obtained further delays and a change of venue to Milledgeville in Baldwin County, two counties south of Greene. The new venue was intended to find a jury away from the emotions then coursing through Tommy Rowry's home county. Greene County Superior Court Judge Joseph Duke would preside in the Milledgeville courthouse, where jury selection was to begin in mid-February, 1980.[45]

Odd developments followed. Wallace's lawyer filed an insanity plea aiming at having him declared unfit to stand trial. After a lengthy hearing, a jury of eleven whites and one black found him competent. Augustine then filed for a continuance that was denied. Finally, on the very morning that jury selection was to commence, Augustine asked that he be permitted to withdraw. Judge Duke instantly denied that as well.[46]

The trial started, and the defense called a psychiatrist from Central State Hospital to testify that Wallace was not capable of malice. The state immediately objected, and the judge ordered the testimony inadmissible because an insanity plea had been ruled out by the earlier hearing on that issue. Augustine told reporters during a recess that there was no other defense he could argue other than insanity, and so that was pretty much it for the trial. The next day, the jury brought in a guilty verdict, and Wallace was subsequently sentenced to death for murder, 20 years for aggravated assault, seven years for theft, and one year for drunk driving.[47]

As do all death-row inmates, Wallace started appealing the verdict in state courts, exhausting that route on September 30, 1981, when the Georgia Supreme Court declared that the "appellant's sentence to death for murder is not excessive or disproportionate" for the crime he committed. The court specifically found that the state had adequately countered the defense's motion regarding insanity.

Next came the federal *habeas corpus* appeals, where it proceeded from the Federal District Court of Middle Georgia to the higher U.S. Court of Appeals for the Eleventh Circuit in Atlanta. This took a while, but Wallace's new attorneys eventually hit pay dirt when the courts decided that insufficient attention had been given to the insanity plea evidence. In March 1985, the Eleventh Circuit overturned the guilty verdict and ordered a new trial. Trial finally commenced in June 1987 with the jury composition reversed from the first time around, i.e. to eleven blacks and one white.[48]

At this point, things took an unexpected turn. Fully expecting the new defense to capitalize on the Eleventh Circuit's decision regarding the original insanity plea, the court was stunned when Wallace's lawyer announced that his client was "completely sane" and ready after all this time to finally be able to tell a jury what really happened on that spring night in Union Point eight years ago. Wallace took the stand in his own defense, a rare and risky venture in a capital case.

Under questioning by his attorney, Wallace painted a picture wherein Rowry and Cook had been rough with him, a treatment that culminated when they got him in City Hall and Rowry went at him with his blackjack, hitting him twice in the head. During this vicious attack, Cook had pulled out his gun. Fearing for his life, Wallace went for the gun, which went off. The one bullet struck both officers. Forensic evidence was presented to show that the weapon had only been fired once instead of multiple times as maintained at the previous trial. Insanity was not the issue. It was now a self-defense case.

The jury bought it and came back after two hours with a not-guilty verdict on everything except the drunk-driving charge for which he was sentenced to time served. Released from prison, he had no further legal troubles. Ironically, Wallace's mental condition, presumably not an issue in the killing of Tommy Rowry, deteriorated and completely incapacitated him by the late 1990s.[49]

On May 20, 1979, four days after he was killed, funeral services were held for Tommy Rowry. The turnout was enormous, so large that the Union Point gymnasium was needed as the venue. The place was filled almost equally with black and white faces. Some 75 police officers from all over were present to pay respects to their fellow fallen officer. A long line of their patrol cars would escort the hearse to the cemetery at the Mount Pleasant Baptist Church there in Union Point.

At the family's request, the principal remarks in memoriam to Thomas Rowry, Jr. were delivered by the man who had hired him as a police officer, Union Point Chief of Police Carlton Lewis.

Later that night, Carlton and Eleanor were having supper alone at home. They both had been quiet after returning from the funeral, and both had so far been moving food around their plates without eating much of it.

"Those were lovely words you said for Tommy, Carlton. They really were."

"I didn't know what I was going to say until I got up there."

"You didn't need to, you let your heart speak for you. Everybody knew that."

"I just can't get over how the situation went from routine to Tommy being dead in a heartbeat. And, the thought of him staggering down the street with all that blood..." Carlton paused and coughed softly. "...that won't ever go away. Or my worry for his wife and that baby boy of theirs. What are they going to do without him?"

Eleanor did not respond. She just sat staring at her husband.

"What are you thinking, Hon?" he finally asked her.

She swallowed, and her eyes misted.

"I'm thinking it could have been you, Carlton."

She choked back a sob.

"Someday, it may be you."

Chap 13 — Miss Eleanor's Courage

The love of Carlton Lewis's life was Eleanor Jones, who he met after the war while in the dry-cleaning business. She had graduated from the Georgia State College for Women[50] in Milledgeville with a degree in secondary education and landed a job teaching home economics in Union Point where she boarded with another teacher and her husband. Carlton noticed her one day, perhaps due to her red hair, and, with his characteristic self-confidence, promptly asked her out. Her hometown was Norwood, a drive-through town with a population of just a few hundred people about 25 miles southeast of Union Point in Warren County. She would spend weekends there with her family, and so Carlton drove over to Norwood to pick her up for their first date. When he was let into her parents' home, Eleanor's father gave him a long and thorough eyeballing before releasing his daughter into his temporary care. The inspection was of sufficient duration to silently but clearly pass along a father's warning about how his daughter had better be treated. Carlton got that message, and he took her to eat at the little restaurant in Warrenton, the county seat just a few miles from tiny Norwood.

Carlton Lewis knew right away that Eleanor was the girl for him. They dated only a few months before marrying in March 1946 as Baptists in Norwood's Methodist church, which a Baptist congregation shared for lack of their own building at the time. Carlton was 30 and Eleanor 24 the year they married. Their son Tom, who was to be an only child, would come along in 1951.

Whereas Carlton was famously outgoing – he never met a stranger and loved everybody he met – Eleanor was far more reserved. She was a schoolteacher, plain and simple. Teaching was her life at the end of which she would have taught school for 39 years. Her whole focus was on her family, her school children, and her Church. Not much else mattered to her. Carlton used to make Tom laugh at the dinner table by asking his wife how much she made as a school teacher. "Well," she'd reply, "I guess I don't really know." In fact, when Carlton went into policing, Eleanor was the major breadwinner.

To the family, Eleanor was known as "Pie," derived from a comment her father had made about her being "as sweet as pie." Her brother C. A. started calling her Pie after that, and the nickname stuck. It was restricted, however, for family use only and remained unknown to her students, fellow teachers, and even the members of her church.

Eleanor was born April 13, 1922 to Claude Alexander Jones and his wife Martha Adelaide Hughes, who went by Addie. Eleanor was the youngest of their three children – Emmie Elizabeth, who also became a school teacher, and Claude, Jr., invariably known as C. A. and who would become prosperous with a number of enterprises in Atlanta. Claude, Sr. began as a farmer, but by 1940 was a traveling salesman of men's suits. His wife was a seamstress, a talent passed along to Eleanor which she used for the rest of her life, sometimes to earn a little money on the side. Eleanor's father and mother would die in 1957 and 1958.[51] C. A., who helped Eleanor through college, and Emmie would both survive their little sister by well over a decade.

When the Greene County schools consolidated with smaller city schools, Eleanor knew she would have to switch to Greene County High School. So that she could remain in Union Point, she got a second degree, this time in elementary education from the University of Georgia. After many years of teaching high school home economics and health, she retooled as a fifth-grade teacher. Regardless of her grade level, to her students she was always "Miss Eleanor."

Eleanor and Carlton brought up their son in a strict Southern Baptist household. They were both very involved in their church. In addition to Carlton being a deacon, they jointly served as treasurers for 25 years. She, of course, did the real work in that position. Every Sunday after church, they would take the donation proceeds home, count it up, and roll the coins. Must churches would have two families do this, but because he was the police chief and she was a revered teacher, they were considered inherently trustworthy. Carlton would take the money to the bank on Monday mornings.

As good Baptists are, they were teetotalers. Carlton had smoked Pall Malls much of his life, but he put them down along with his drinking a month before little Tommy was born. Eleanor could be very strict with their son, while Carlton, the police officer who had seen too many young people run wild, was the lenient one. Sometimes Carlton would make his point indirectly such as in the case of not imposing a curfew when Tom was in high school. He clarified the apparently lax decision to Tom.

"Son, you don't have to be home at midnight. I've picked up too many teenagers off the highway that were killed driving too fast trying to get home to meet a curfew." Tom later concluded that his dad realized that if everybody else had a curfew, including the girl he was with, then what was Tom going to do. More than once would Carlton get his point across by explaining things in similar context. It worked.

On other occasions, Carlton could be a real hardliner. He would tell Tom that he'd better never catch him doing something or other in a tone of voice that made Tom wonder if his dad might reach across and give him a good whack of preventive discipline. Once when he was debating some point with his dad he was shut down when told that "If I tell you black's white, then black is white. There's no debate about that." Such was Carlton's self confidence in his own judgement of a world about which he was not lacking in opinions.

Nevertheless, Carlton was also very kind and generous with Tom. When he was still in high school, Carlton gave him an old Fairlane 500 along with permission to drive the car down to Daytona Beach on spring break. That adventure was a long-standing tradition for Southern high school juniors of both sexes, causing anxiety in countless parents in anticipation of that potentially risky venture into independence. While doing his night-before packing in prep for the morning departure, Tom often recalls his father coming into his room saying he wanted to talk, something the younger Lewis was not at all surprised to hear.

"Look, son, your Mother and I gave you our permission to go down to Daytona because we know you'll do the right thing."

Tommy braced himself for a long discussion about just what constituted the "right thing." But there would be no drawn-out series of warnings – just a short pause.

"I want you to remember something."

"Yes, Sir."

"It takes a lifetime to build a reputation, but only three minutes to destroy it."

That was it – a clear statement covering all the traps one could fall into that Tom, indeed, never forgot.

A year and a half later on the day Tom went off to college at Georgia Southern in Statesboro, he was once again loading up the Fairlane. His mother planned to take the two-hour drive down there with him to help settle him into his dorm room, but his father had said, "No, you're going off to college. You don't need me for that." He further advised his son with another of his one-liners, "Don't let your studies interfere with your education."

With what they had made and put aside in a small college account, Carlton and Eleanor could put him through college with Tom working just a small amount during holidays, breaks, and summers. When he was a junior at Georgia Southern and came home during a break, Tom's father asked him what car he particularly liked.

Tom's immediate reply was, "Have you ever seen one of those new Monte Carlos?! Gosh, they are beautiful!

"Those are nice," Carlton replied. "Which model do you like?"

"Gold with a black vinyl top. Those are really sharp!" Tom said enthusiastically.

When Tom came home in the Fairlane at the next break and rounded the corner to their house, there before him in their driveway was a gold and black, brand-new Monte Carlo. Carlton, who had been on the lookout for him from the window came out.

"You like that, Tommy? It's yours!"

On the dash was a gold plate that said, "Personal Property of Tom Lewis."

That account they had saved for his education had done well, and enough was left over for the car. Tom and Patty kept the Monte Carlo and eventually put more than 150,000 miles on it.

As an adult, Tom Lewis came to realize how saintly his mother was. How else could she put up with all that went with Carlton's job, significantly amplified by his personality and life-threatening tendency towards risk taking? The late hours, the uncertainty as to his safety at any given time, and the days away from home staked out at some liquor still in the boonies all took their toll. The fear of a dire phone call regarding her husband never left the back of her mind.

Eleanor was a quiet person who did not like a lot of attention. She never discussed her fears for her husband's life and bottled up her worries and stress to her own detriment. As the years went on, she would occasionally bring up the issue of his retirement with Carlton, occasionally revealing her deep concern with a tearful plea over the ever-increasing risk of his job that went with advancing age.

She doted on Carlton and was at his beck and call. Even before he became a policeman, he depended upon her for everything. When he had the Sinclair station, she would fix a full meal, put it on a plate, and drive down to the station to take it to him during the summer when she wasn't working. He adored her and did not consciously take advantage of her return love for him. Her devotion just seemed natural to them both.

Once when Tom and his wife Patty were having dinner in Union Point with Carlton and Eleanor, Eleanor was putting away dishes in the kitchen after clearing the table when Carlton picked up his iced-tea glass and shook it, rattling the ice. Eleanor hurried back into the dining room to refill his glass. Patty slowly turned her gaze to Tom and gave him that "don't-you-ever-do-that-to-me" look, which she repeated in words on their drive back to Atlanta that night.

After Carlton died, several people came up to Tom and told him that they wish his dad could have lived longer, but, had his mother gone first, Carlton could never have made it. He was so totally dependent on her, and they were right. He looked to her for everything, and she took care of everything. That's just the way it was.

Etched into Tom's memory is the conversation at the dinner table one evening in the mid-1960s that was low-key as usual. He would later realize that what was said that night spoke volumes to his parents' regard for their role in the community and its response to the hammer that was being dropped on many Southern locales to force compliance with new civil rights laws.

As was their ritual following a brief saying of grace, they would go around the table and each would in turn talk about their day. Tom would go first, then Carlton, and Eleanor would finish it off. Tom would talk about something, often funny, that happened at school;

Carlton would give the highlights of police activity while always omitting the bad stuff; and, Eleanor would typically say it was just a typical day and leave it at that. But, this night was different.

When it came her turn, she wiped her lips with her napkin and returned it to her lap. And, then she told them about her remarkable day.

"Well," she said, glancing in turn at each of them, "the Superintendent called all the teachers together for a meeting after school in the gym."

Carlton, now curious as to what Ford Boston had told his teachers, responded.

"He did? What for? Is he giving everyone raises?"

Ignoring the facetious question, Eleanor proceeded.

"He asked for volunteers."

"For what?" Carlton was getting impatient now. Tom was all ears as well.

"He told us that school desegregation was coming our way, one way or the other. So many places are trying to stand fast against it, but they are only inviting federal troops into their towns to force the inevitable."

She paused, but neither Tom nor his dad said anything to slow her down. So, she continued.

"Ford told us he'd decided we wouldn't wait for that. He said we need to set an example and show the government that we had leaders in this county who make the right decisions and take the right actions without being forced."

Her boys were riveted by now.

"He said we need to move some white teachers to black schools and black teachers to white schools. And, instead of assigning teachers. He was asking for volunteers."

Carlton knew what was coming next.

"So, I raised my hand."

"Anyone else raise theirs?" asked Carlton.

"A teacher from the colored elementary then raised her hand. I expect more ladies will step up soon." For now, though, Eleanor and her black counterpart would be the pioneers who would essentially swap schools. No students would yet be moving across the ancient racial boundary, at least not immediately.

"What do you think about this, Honey?" she asked her husband.

"Well, Hon, I admire you for this, but it'll sure be different," he responded with a truth that she well knew.

That was it – no further discussion ensued. It was as if this monumentally brave action on Eleanor's part was as routine as her volunteering to help out at a PTA meeting.

It was months later and a few days after she started at the black school when Carlton said, with a big grin, that people in town were saying the only reason she volunteered was because of him. She found nothing funny in this.

"Look here, Carlton, I volunteered because that's what I wanted to do. It was my decision and mine alone. You need to tell people that!" she snapped. And that's what Carlton told people thereafter, adding that he was proud of what his wife had done.

One day soon after that, she came home in tears.

"What's wrong, Honey?" Carlton asked. "Did somethin' bad happen today?"

Tom said nothing but stared at his mother for her response.

"I'm just so upset. When I brought my children back from lunch today, I paused for just a second to listen outside Mrs. Young's class across the hall from mine. I was shocked at what I heard her say to those kids."

"Well, what did she say, Honey? Tell me now."

Eleanor gulped and took a deep breath.

"I heard her tell them that Washington, DC was a state just like Georgia and that it was located on the "Poto-matic" River. Can you believe that? What have these kids been taught?!" She gulped again and a tear ran down her cheek. And, then she went on.

"And on top of that, the textbooks are old, hand-me-downs from the white school that are written all over inside and have pages torn out."

Carlton patted her hand and shook his head in understanding.

"And everything was supposed to be 'separate but equal.' That's what we've been told for decades. It's an outright lie!"

With that, Eleanor headed into the kitchen. It was time to fix supper.

But, things soon settled down. That one exceptionally poor teacher was the exception. The other teachers had been reticent around Eleanor the first few days due to their anxiety surrounding her being there. But, they as well as Eleanor soon realized that they all were there for the same purpose – to teach the kids. And they all did their best toward that goal.

And thus transpired a significant instance of personal resolution and action by a brave individual towards righting a wrong that had infected her home state for more than two centuries. Few, if any, other white citizens of Greene County, Georgia, would have, as did Eleanor Lewis, raised their hand that day.

Carlton and Eleanor Lewis in the late 1970s.

Chap 14 — The Honor Guard

Union Point, Monday, March 17, 1986, 3:00 pm

More than fifty police cars from jurisdictions all over the state were arriving to line Thornton Street. After the service, they would escort the hearse from the First Baptist Church to Carlton Lewis's final resting place in Greenlawn Cemetery less than a mile away.

Also arriving were Governor and Mrs. Joe Frank Harris who had flown from Atlanta in a small aircraft and driven by GBI agents from the Greene County Airport to the church. First Lady Elizabeth Harris later told *The Herald-Journal* that "Carlton Lewis will always be special to us. In 1981, when Joe Frank was running for Governor, our children were politicking in Greene County and Carlton Lewis spent a whole day showing them around and introducing them to so many people. And, of course, his son Tommy and his wife are very close friends." The Colonel of the Georgia State Patrol and his top brass along with many of the Governor's department heads were there as well.

The church, among the largest in the county, was filling to overflowing. Among the 500 or so funeral attendees, there was a significant number of people from the black community of Greene County as well as among the ranks of the police officers. White or black, all were there to pay final respects to a man of authority who had said just a few months before that "To make a good policeman, you've got to love people and want to help people. If you see a person take advantage of somebody and you are a good policeman, it makes you mad, it makes you want to take up for 'em, you want to take his place. You have to punish the guilty to take care of the innocent."

✝ ✝ ✝ ✝

A few years earlier, Carlton had reported chest pains to his doctor, who put him on a diet and exercise regimen. Carlton immediately started walking everywhere that was reasonable, which included the mile each way to work and patrol walks through town. He typically did seven miles a day on foot. These walks were a routine fixture in his life and yet another reason why the people of Union Point admired their police chief.

Carlton called Tommy on March 14, 1986, a Friday, in the Governor's Office in Atlanta. He told Tom that he wasn't feeling real good and that he had an appointment with his cardiologist on Monday. Tom told his dad to call his doctor right away. A bit later, Carlton called back to report that the doctor said they would run another stress test on Monday to see what was going on. Plus, he had taken one of his angina pills and was feeling better.

The next day, while out on one of these famous walks on a lovely Ides of March Saturday, Carlton Lewis – retired just two weeks from thirteen years as Union Point's Police Chief – collapsed outside the house of his long-time friends Mary and Harold Finch who lived on, ironically, Carlton Avenue. A massive heart attack had killed him before he hit the sidewalk.

What a tragic irony this must have presented to Eleanor. Her husband had survived 22 years at one of the highest-risk jobs a person can have. He had been beaten up and shot at and countless times had put himself into risk situations that would have terrified the average person. But, he had made it through all that and had finally taken the retirement Eleanor had so long wanted for them. And, then, he drops dead while out on a walk! How could that be? How could God let that happen to them? It must have been nearly unbearable for her.

Union Point and Greene County lost an important figure in their history. Two paragraphs and the closing line in a *Herald-Journal* editorial after the funeral put the community's regard in plain English:

Carlton Lewis policed for over 20 years in Greene County and his reputation was tough but fair. He believed that no one was above the law. He didn't care if your name was John Smith or if you were white or black or the biggest political figure in Greene County. If you were drunk or broke a law he would arrest you and make sure your case would come to court.

He was a man respected by all walks of life. Police work was his life and he served to the day he retired to the best of his ability. He was fair, honest and dedicated and he made the citizens of Greene County an outstanding police officer for the past 22 years.

... We like so many here lost a personal friend with the death of Carlton Lewis.

On the day he was buried, only twelve days had passed since Carlton and Eleanor had been treated to a celebratory retirement dinner hosted by Union Point Mayor Ben Stewart, Jr. Several of his old friends and colleagues spoke of what Carlton had meant to them and their county, and a congratulatory telegram from Governor Harris was read in which the Governor told him, "I appreciate your friendship and wish you every happiness in the coming years."

The Governor had also issued an official state proclamation in which he lauded Carlton's achievements and congratulated him "on his retirement after many years of eminent public service and do further commend him for the valuable contributions he has made to law enforcement and to the well-being of his community."

Carlton's old business partner and former mayor Ben Stewart, Sr. was among those who reminisced about his past association with the honoree. It was with John that Carlton had entered the dry-cleaning business before the war, and they had named their enterprise L. & S. Dry Cleaners. John was also best man at Carlton's and Eleanor's wedding. In his remarks, John remembered "one time when this lady sent her braded rug to be cleaned and when Carlton returned it in a paper bag, it was one big long pony tail. This tickled me but it wasn't too funny to this lady. She was my mama."

They both went away for wartime service and, not long after returning, Carlton left dry cleaning in favor of his subsequent business ventures. In each of these he was successful but unsatisfied until finding his life's calling in law enforcement. Ben recalled for the dinner guests that when a mutual friend asked Carlton how he liked his new role, Carlton replied, "Well, the pay is good and the hours aren't bad, but what I like the most is that the customer is always wrong!"

Eleanor Lewis was escorted into the church by their only child Tom, or Tommy as he is still known by many in Greene County. Some thirty State Patrol Officers were lined along the walkway and up the steps to the packed church. As Tom took his mother to the front pew, they saw the Macon Georgia Police Department's Honor Guard standing at attention by the casket. They were in full-dress uniform, their sidearms holstered on their polished leather belt harnesses.

When she saw those guns on the honor guard, Eleanor turned to Tom and said, "I don't want them up there."

"Mother, this is an honor for Daddy to have them here," Tom explained.

Emphatically, she replied, "I don't want anybody with guns standing around that casket." No further discussion would be allowed.

Tom stopped and gestured for one of the ushers.

"Go up and tell them to sit down," he said with a nod in the direction of the honor guard.

"Are you sure, Tommy?" the man asked with wide eyes.

"She's asked for that, and that's what she's going to get."

Eleanor Lewis had always proudly supported Carlton in his police work, but she had been through so many terrifying instances when severe injury or death could just have easily taken her husband from her at an even earlier age. She simply could not abide having guns – the symbol of all that could have happened to Carlton during his two decades of policing – as a part of her last few minutes with her husband.

They waited until the guard had retired to the pews before Eleanor was ready to continue to her seat. The service could now begin.

The sanctuary of the First Baptist Church was filled with solemn processional music as the family filed in. Tom escorted his mother on whom all eyes were focused. Patty, walking behind her mother-in-law, held the hands of Wes and Ellen. Tom's six aunts and their families expanded the contingent considerably, but it was nothing compared to the number of family friends and admirers of Chief Lewis who came to bid him goodbye and pay their respects to Eleanor.

The Reverend Clyde Hampton rose and walked slowly to the pulpit to carry out his role as the officiant. The order of worship for Carlton's service was traditional with prayers, readings from scripture, and songs from a choir who dearly missed their long-time fellow member. When the time came for the pastor to deliver the eulogy, he began with what Carlton meant to the people of Union Point whom he had watchfully protected for thirteen years. Rev. Hampton described his service to Greene County during his years as a deputy for L. L. Wyatt, who had grown increasingly reliant on Carlton in his last years as Sheriff. The Reverend went back in time to Carlton's World War II service, which followed his looking after his sisters Willie May, Agnes, and Edith while three of them worked in the hosiery with Edith still in school, his productiveness in the community following the War, and his early leadership involvement in their church. He then spoke of the wonderful marriage and love between Carlton and Eleanor and how between the two of them – he as a policeman and she as a teacher – they had bettered the lives of countless Greene Countians.

Pastor Hampton then addressed Carlton's religious faith.

"Carlton Lewis was more than a Chief or a Deputy, he was a strong and dedicated Christian man. He was one of the finest Christian men I have had the pleasure to know. He was a rock in our beloved Church."

He turned to Eleanor. "Your dear husband has now hung up his holster and gun for the final time. He will never need them again. There are no bad people in heaven."

When she lost her husband that spring of 1986, Eleanor lost the central focus of her life. She had loved teaching and cherished each of the children she had nurtured over the years, but the pleasure in that vanished along with Carlton. She wanted to quit teaching immediately, but Tom talked her out of quitting in mid-year. It would dishonor her distinguished career by abandoning her children and school like that. Besides, her husband would have vigorously opposed it. So, Miss Eleanor stuck with it, but she informed the Superintendent of her retirement at the end of the 1985-86 school year.

Ed Corry, who had replaced Ford Boston as Superintendent, wrote Eleanor a letter dated April 7, 1986 that included the words: "At a time in your life when I want to wish you much happiness and joy, I know that you are devastated by Carlton's death. I feel I cannot adequately express my sympathy on the passing of Carlton. He and I enjoyed many good hunting trips and happy times together and I shall miss him also."

The Herald-Journal reported on Eleanor's retirement on June 13, 1986 in an article that described a celebration held for her at Union Point Elementary School the prior week. She was reported as surprised by the luncheon and to see Tom and his family, her sister Emmie, and many friends there in addition to her students and fellow teachers. The principal gave her a plaque, Patty Lewis read a proclamation from Gov. Harris, and her students gave her a basket full of gifts. The article closed with, *"'Miss Eleanor' is a very fine, professional teacher and we all express our thanks for all that she has given to us and the children of Greene County."*

One can only wonder what Eleanor was thinking during this party in her honor. Having set aside her career of 38 years, her life would now be even emptier. Depression had already set in, and she soon began to show signs of dementia that was diagnosed as Alzheimer's Disease. She went to live with her sister Emmie, who kept Tom apprised of his mother's decline in between his frequent trips from Atlanta to see her during her remaining months. She grew less and less cognizant of her surroundings and finally no longer recognized even her Tommy. Emmie suspected something else was wrong with her, and a visit to Dr. Billy Rhodes in Union Point led to tests that showed Eleanor had terminal cancer on top of all her other problems. One effect on her brain from the Alzheimer's was the masking of pain from the cancer.

Eleanor died on December 16, 1988, two years and nine months after Carlton's passing. She was 66 years old. The years of bottled-up stress from constant worry over her husband's safety had taken a terrible toll, but Eleanor was now once again at her beloved husband's side in Greenlawn Cemetery.

Carlton's funeral had been awash in a sea of flowers. Their disposition presented a huge challenge mostly solved through gifts to local retirement and nursing homes. It seemed like such a waste of money. Knowing of the limited time ahead for his mother, Tom and Patty decided prior to her death that it would be an appropriate memorial to her to set up a scholarship in her name initially funded by donations in lieu of flowers when she passed away and supplemented by additional gifts from family members. Thus, the Eleanor Lewis Scholarship Fund now annually awards scholarships to young people of the Union Point First Baptist Church thereby acknowledging Eleanor's love for education as well as for the Church she and Carlton had served so faithfully.

Chap 15 — Assessing Carlton Lewis

The Thirteenth Amendment to the United States Constitution (Ratified December 6, 1865) reads: *Neither slavery nor involuntary servitude, except as a punishment for crime whereof the party shall have been duly convicted, shall exist within the United States, or any place subject to their jurisdiction.*

Perhaps there is a parallel universe in which John Wilkes Booth changed his mind at the last minute, Andrew Johnson did not become president, reconstruction was never imposed on the South, and the Thirteenth Amendment was expanded at the outset to state that all persons freed from slavery were citizens who enjoyed all the rights laid out in the U.S. Constitution. And, one more thing – every white citizen of the land took that amendment to heart.

This is, of course, naïve and wishful thinking about the malleability of human nature. While the former Confederate states could do nothing about the Thirteenth Amendment, they were determined to ensure that black Americans would never be assimilated as full-blown citizens.

As a Tennessee senator, Johnson opposed secession and remained in the national capital when his home state withdrew from the Union. As President, he adopted Lincoln's lenient reconstruction policies and let the defeated rebellious states control their own elections and return confiscated land to the original owners that had been distributed to freed slaves. Former prominent Confederates, who might have been hanged had Lincoln's Secretary of War Edwin Stanton had his way under Johnson, showed up as elected members of Congress. Except for the 620,000 Americans killed in the Civil War, it was as if those 49 months of terrible conflict had never happened.

President Johnson's approach to Reconstruction encouraged some of those states to pass "black codes" intended to define the role of freed blacks as a separate labor class. A particularly popular feature of these codes were vagrancy laws in which freed people could be arrested for next to nothing and sentenced to involuntary and uncompensated labor. Governments would then lease their labor to landowners, and there you have it – a new kind of slavery. It was all very clever, but the reaction from northern states and the U.S. Congress resulted in the imposition of Radical Reconstruction on the South. It also led to Johnson being impeached by the House of Representatives in early 1868 and promptly tried in the Senate.

Johnson avoided Senate conviction by a single vote, but, never mind, the reconstruction pendulum had already swung the other way when a new Congress controlled by radical Republicans, elected by a nation that had soured on their President, re-convened in December 1865. Among a number of civil rights actions, Congress set out to implement another Reconstruction amendment to the Constitution – the Fourteenth (ratified in July 1868) – that goes far beyond the Thirteenth Amendment's elimination of slavery to make freed slaves citizens of the U.S. The 14th also requires that the states protect the rights of citizens to life, liberty, and property under legislated law – the "Due Process Clause." It also included the "Equal Protection Clause" requiring states to treat all people under their jurisdiction – even non-citizens – equally under the law. Thereafter followed the Fifteenth Amendment (February 1870), which fully franchised former slaves as voters. A powerful constitutional framework was in place, presumably to ensure the rights of freed slaves as full citizens of the United States. But, it took another century and a change in societal attitudes to finally give full rights and the franchise to African Americans.[52]

Those Confederates sent to Congress under Johnson's magnanimous Reconstruction principles were replaced by men who had been slaves, and the South found itself descended upon by "Carpetbaggers" and under federal military rule lasting into 1877 when Congress effectively put an end to Reconstruction. There began a new process for keeping the constitutionally mandated rights outside the grasp of their intended recipients.

For the ensuing 87 years, Jim Crow, including beefed-up vagrancy laws, continued in the South and more or less successfully set back the clock to keep blacks under the yoke in spite of the Constitution. Ironically, the Jim Crow era equaled the interval from the Nation's founding in 1776 to the Emancipation Proclamation.[53]

In 1964, a different President Johnson pushed a new Civil Rights Act through Congress. *Brown v. Board of Education* had been decided ten years earlier under the 14th Amendments Equal Protection Clause, but segregated schools were still firmly in place as the "separate but equal" illusion strategy of the South's old guard continued unabated. The problem with *Brown* was that it set no timetable for desegregation, only requiring the process go forward "with all deliberate speed," whatever that meant. The 1964 Civil Rights Act, which held a federal dollars stick over the South, was the true beginning of the end for segregation, and, thus, 1964 can be regarded as the end of Jim Crow.

And, of course, 1964 was the very year in which Carlton Lewis became a policeman. When Carlton was born in 1916, a slave child born in 1860 would have been 66 years old. It seems probable that there were former slaves living in Greene County when Carlton was a child. A few of these could have been descendants of the four slaves once owned by his grandfather William. They would have likely carried the surname of Lewis.

Carlton had grown from infancy to maturity in a South in which Jim Crow legislation had kept "the Negro in his place." Separate neighborhoods, separate schools, separate water fountains, separate cemeteries, separate restaurants, the back of the bus, literacy tests, and the widespread use by whites of what is now called the "N-word" were among many other features of a discriminatory society at the foundation of Carlton's everyday life.

So, was Carlton prejudiced towards blacks? The answer is simple – of course he was. How could he not be? The deeper and more important question is how did he personally regard black citizens of his community, and, most critically, how did he treat them as a policeman?

The Union Point Police Department ca. 1982.

✚ ✚ ✚ ✚

Union Point, Early Friday afternoon, February 14, 1985

Their after-lunch conversation had died down while they lingered over two extra cups of coffee Beatrice had brewed fresh just for them. The good coffee came on top of an even-better blue plate special of fried pork chops with rice and lima beans. When nothing but bones were left on their plates, the owner of Huff's appeared at their table with two big bowls of banana pudding.

Ellis's eyes went wide at the sight and then settled on her smiling face.

"What's goin' on here, Beatrice. Have you gone overboard on your meds today?"

"Hah, that's a good one, Ellis. No, I haven't gotten too deep in the pills today, or ever, if it's any of your business. I was just thinking about how you two've been comin' her near forever. Why you and the Chief here are my best customers, Judge, and I just want to give you two a little thank you. Plus, if you'd slowed down to read the sign on my door when you came in to put the feed bags on, you'd have seen that I'm closed all next week. I'm kinda lookin' forward to that."

"Closed?!" Carlton let out. Ellis just stared at her, stunned by this revelation.

"Yep, Judy's goin' to have that baby Monday by C-section, and she told me she wanted her mama there with her. So, I'm off to Valdosta for the big event. Henry's gonna stay here to take care of the chickens, but he can't run no restaurant."

"No argument there, Beatrice," said Carlton.

Ellis took another approach to the revelation.

"What's made you happier, Beatrice, seeing that new grandbaby come into the world or leaving Henry here by his lonesome?"

Beatrice grinned at them, spun on her heals and headed for the kitchen while tossing back, "Well, I'll just have to think about that, boys."

Ten minutes later, the pudding and coffee were both gone. Carlton put down his napkin and said, "Well, I'd best head back to the fort. It's been quiet so far today, but things can always break loose."

"Mind if I tag along?" asked Ellis.

"Sure," replied a startled Carlton. "Somethin' up you need to talk about?"

"Nothin' I 'need' to talk about."

Once outside Huff's Diner, the two old friends crossed Lamb avenue and headed for City Hall, half a block up Scott.

As they walked by Walker's filling station, Ellis remarked in a quiet tone, "You know, I can't go by here without thinking about poor Tommy dying back there by those gas pumps after being shot in the very building we're headed for now."

"Me neither," Carlton replied.

✢ ✢ ✢ ✢

They continued toward City Hall in silence, which held until they were entering Carlton's office.

"How about a Coke?" Carlton asked Ellis.

"Now, that'd be nice, Carlton. Thanks."

With bottles of Coca Cola in hand, they settled into the two upholstered chairs Carlton crammed into a corner of his small domain for just such occasions.

"What you got on your mind, Judge? I'm always glad to talk with you, but you're not usually so sociable. Are you okay?"

"I'm as fine as a man my age can rightfully be, I suppose. But, I'm not so sure about you."

"What! Why do you say that?" asked a surprised Carlton.

"Look, Chief, I know I've got a decade and a half on you, but you ain't no spring chicken. You're turning 70 in a couple of months. You're too old for this job."

"You been talkin' to Eleanor, Judge?"

"Don't need to. I know you've still got what it takes between the ears to be Chief, but what are you going to do the next time you pull some fella over and he gets the jump on you? You're just not the fighter you used to be."

Taking a sip of Coke, Ellis paused for a reaction. He got only a stare.

"Let me rephrase that – have you ever thought about what it will do to Eleanor when one of your officers comes to your front door to tell her you've been killed in a drunk-driver stop?"

Another pause and another stare while Ellis took a second sip from his Coke bottle.

Carlton got up and walked over to stand by his desk.

"Sure, I've thought of that. And, Eleanor is bringing it up more and more often. I know I've got to quit. I just wished it'd been thirty-five or forty years of policing instead of twenty-two. It's gone by so dog-gone fast!"

"We can always want more, but we have to be thoughtful and grateful for what the Lord has given us. You just can't take the risk to ask Him for more."

Ellis continued.

"But, let's look at it from another direction. How do you feel about your performance on the job?"

"Well, I've put a lot of bad people behind bars. And, I'm not aware of any of them not being guilty of their crime."

"I know that's right, Carlton, but I'm talkin' something more fundamental here. What I'm really getting at is do you believe you've done your job not just effectively, but – and this is even more important in the long run – have you done it fairly."

"I'm not sure that's my call, Ellis. What do you think?"

"What percentage of the people you've arrested have been black?"

"Probably three-fourths of them, I guess. Why?"

Ignoring Carlton's one-word question, Ellis kept going.

"And what percentage of the men you've fought have been black?"

With no hesitation, Carlton said, "Near eighty percent, I'd estimate."

"Why is that, Carlton? Are only blacks violent?

"No, of course not. Look here, Ellis, you got to understand something. I've enjoyed every minute I've had of policing. I've seen lots of things, and I've helped lots of folks. I've pulled through lots of different situations, but I have always had a drive inside me to do that – to help people at the same time as I'm enforcing the law."

Carlton stopped momentarily to take to his chair again before going on.

"Ellis, I believe that to make a good policeman you've got to love people, you've got to want to help people. If a person takes advantage of somebody, if you are a good policeman, it makes you mad and you want to take up for them. You want to take his place and then you have ambitions to punish the guilty so you can take care of the innocent. It don't matter if that person is white or black or polka dotted. We all need help. We all need somebody to step up for us sometimes."

The judge leaned forward and looked intently at Carlton.

"I knew you'd say something along those lines, old friend. But, why is it mostly blacks you have your famous 'tussles' with?"

"It's clear as the back of my hand to me, Judge."

"Then explain it to me," Ellis replied.

"It must be obvious to you, too, that they get into trouble cause most of them don't have nothin' else to do."

"And, why's that?" Ellis asked even though he knew the answer.

"Because we whites won't give them jobs. Just look at the sock mill."

That was precisely the direction Ellis would have gone with had Carlton needed some help with the answer. But, he didn't. They both knew that throughout much of the 20th century, Greene County, like many other rural Southern locales, benefitted from the growth of the textile industry. Jobs in plants like the Union Manufacturing sock facility in Union Point did not require much skill or education. Logic would dictate that company management would take maximum advantage of the available labor pool to keep wages down and profits up. But, until 1964 only about 2% of textile workers were black, and they tended to be given the most menial jobs in the plant.[54] As a result, black unemployment was pervasive, which, as it tends to do in all racial and ethnic subgroups, leads to getting in trouble with the police. Alcohol often figured into the encounters, and much of the ensuring violence Carlton Lewis engaged in during arrests was with blacks who were typically young and often drunk.

The phone rang. Carlton picked it up. Ellis could tell it was Eleanor, and that she was probably just confirming when Carlton would be home for supper.

"Don't know for sure, Hon. The Judge came back with me after lunch, and we're just sittin' here talkin'."

Carlton went silent for a while, listening to his wife.

"Thanks, Hon. I'll give you a call when I'm ready to step out the door."

The call ended when Carlton replied back to her, "Love you too, Hon."

He put the phone back on the receiver, turned and said to Ellis, "Now, you aren't in some kind of conspiracy with my wife, are you, Your Honor?"

Ellis chuckled, "I should be and should have started it long ago, but, no, I'm a lone wolf on this one, Chief."

While Carlton was talking with Eleanor, Ellis's thoughts wandered back to the fighting aspects of Carlton's profession. He knew that a police officer had to be prepared to fight, to go hand-to-hand with drunks, with people who resist arrest, with people who may want to kill him rather than be sent off to prison. He also knew that an officer couldn't sit back and expect someone else to take care of a situation.

Ellis knew that Carlton was born to this line of work. He had an inherent fearlessness – a willingness approaching a desire to jump headlong into the fray. Carlton entered the world with those traits, which were later honed by the training he received when he went off to war in the Navy.

Ellis had heard about Carlton's military experience on more than one occasion, but he knew Carlton enjoyed recalling that episode in his life. So, Ellis got the conversation back on track after the phone call by asking Carlton about his Navy training.

Carlton complied with, "Well, I went in and they trained me to fight. They trained me how you should fight, how you control yourself, how you should have a temper, but it's no good unless you control it. Regardless of how scared you get you're supposed to have enough guts and ambition to want to stay there and fight. That's really where, like I say, my life began."

"All that's why Sheriff Wyatt hired you back in '64, isn't it?"

"Well, in those days, Ellis, you didn't have much of a police force. They had one sheriff and normally two deputies. They only had one deputy at that time, and they asked me would I consider. I was not all that rough, but they knew all of my background in the service and everything. They knew I was honest and straight. I go to the church a Christian, which of course you know, and yet I have that Christian drive to take care of people. So that is how I got into it, and there were seventeen others that had their applications in."

"I always figured you did it for the money," Ellis joked.

Carlton laughed, "Come on, now, Judge. You know I took a half salary against what I had been making when I took this job, but I was satisfied because I was doing something I wanted to do and enjoyed doing. When we got up every morning I didn't know whether I was going to Atlanta or whether I was going to Reidsville, or whether we were going to run the prison that day with dogs or what. Every day was a new day, and that is what I enjoyed."

"You worked long hours back then compared to now, didn't you?"

Carlton nodded and then recalled what it was like.

"There ain't much to it now, but back in those days we were working 12 or 15 hours a night. I'd work all during the day and maybe patrol 'til midnight. I've then gone home many a night at twelve and then to bed, but there would be some fight somewhere going on in the county and I can hear Sheriff Wyatt now – he talked so easy, you remember – 'Carlton, go down to (somewhere), they're having a hot supper down there and one man done got cut all to pieces, go in there and check on them. See what's wrong.' Sheriff was 73 years old, and he stayed in the hospital the last four or five years more than he done anything, so all the work was done by me as the chief deputy."

Carlton was on a roll, which was exactly what Ellis wanted him to do. He hoped that in thinking about the past Carlton would get a clearer perspective on the present and, especially, on the future. All Ellis had to do was to suggest a new topic, and Carlton would continue talking, remembering, and – hopefully – assessing.

"On top of all that, I know you took major responsibility for training new deputies."

"I bet you I trained 50 or 100 policemen. They'd go to a police academy, but that's not training them. The sheriff trained me. Back then you didn't have to go to a police academy, but I've been to school. The only thing police academies tell you, they just show you about your rights and the citizen's rights. They don't train a man."

Carlton elaborated.

"I remember calling up to the police academy – all of them there are good friends – and I said, 'I'm sending you a man up there. I don't know whether he's gonna make a policeman or not. I want you to take him and make a policeman out of him.' He said, 'Carlton, I don't take a man and make a policeman out of him. You send me a policeman and I'll help you train him.' That's about right. You don't make a policeman. A good policeman is born and not made. It's got to be in you. You've got to want to do it. You've got to have it in you to want to look after people. You've got to want to help folks. It makes me mad to see anybody just run over somebody else or take advantage of another person. That's got to be in you, back in those days, before you could be a policeman."

"Do any of those men you trained stand out to you?"

"Oh, yeah, several of them were and still are really fine policemen. But, Johnny Grimes was a special standout. He's really climbing up the chain of command in the State Patrol. No tellin' how far up he'll go. I'm really proud of Johnny! We sure had some good times while he was ridin' with me."

Ellis chuckled, "I'll bet you did."

Time for Ellis to steer things in another direction.

"How do you feel about that time the feds investigated you for brutality against blacks?"

Carlton was thoughtful and then replied at length.

"Well, it was two black boys. They were brothers out riding around and trying to pick up some girls. They were drunk. They called me down there, and when I got to the house, I got out of the car and there was two of them all by themselves. Back in those days, we didn't have a partition in our cars. So, I took one of the boys, and he resisted arrest. I manhandled him you know. Like you said, I was a lot younger then. I had thrown him back there in the backseat and got out of the car to get the other one and, man, he was giving me fits. While I was fighting with him, the one in the back seat jumped out of the car and went to running down towards the woods. I shot over his head and told him to stop. He kept going. When he did, I hit this one upside the head because he'd done popped me two or three times."

"Sounds like things were headed for real trouble. What happened next?" Ellis interjected.

"Well, their mama come running down off the back porch. She

140

said 'Heeey, you done shot one and are beatin' the other one to death.' She was just having a durn hissy, and I carried this one down to the jail and locked him up. I went back that night to the house – I knew the other boy'd be there. So, the dad was in the yard when I got there, and I told him I had to go in and get his other boy. He said, 'Okay,' and that's how I locked up the other brother, too."

"Just how is all this police brutality? Sounds to me like you were just doing your job."

Carlton nodded in agreement.

"What happened next was this. A man from up north was runnin' the country club, and one of these boys had been working there. So, he called the U.S. attorney in Washington and told him that I was just picking on all the blacks for no reason except I was prejudiced towards them. So, the Washington man wrote it up and called the FBI down here in Athens and told them to check it out. That FBI agent was all over Greene County interviewing everybody to try to see what in the world he could get on me. After that, he went to the sheriff's office and told Sheriff Wyatt, 'I am going to have to interview Carlton, but you can stay.'"

"And, did Wyatt stay?" Ellis asked.

"Of course, he did. We all sat down in his office, and the FBI man was starting to question me, and I said, 'What's all this about.' He told me. Then I said, 'Did they tell you about how they beat me up and all that. They didn't tell you about that, did they? I was just taking advantage of them, right?'"

"How'd he react to that?"

"It wasn't just what I said to that FBI man since he'd questioned a lot of Greene County black folks and didn't come up with anything. He didn't tell me about that then, but the questioning in Sheriff's office sure didn't last long."

"And that was it? They were done with you?"

"What happened next was that he made out a report and sent it in. I had to wait about a month and finally got an official decision letter sayin' that I hadn't used no more force than was necessary. So, I was cleared on it."

"Well, they sure tried to nail you, didn't they?"

Carlton was about to agree when the phone rang.

When he put it down, Carlton stood up.

"Got to go. A couple of suspicious fellas are in the Stop-N-Go, and making the clerk nervous," Carlton explained.

"Be careful, you hear me," Ellis urged.

"Always," Carlton replied, walking toward the door.

"And, hey, Carlton! Breakfast, 0700 tomorrow mornin'. Huff's. Okay? We need to keep talkin'."

Without slowing down, Carlton nodded in the affirmative.

"0700 it is, Judge." And then he was off to respond to the call.

As the phone rang, Ellis looked at his wrist watch. It was 9:45.

"Now who in the world...," he mumbled as he got up to answer the call.

"That you, Judge?" It was Carlton's recognizable voice.

"It's me, Chief. What's up? Everything okay at the Stop-N-Go?"

"Just a few black boys takin' the back roads from Athens over to Augusta buyin' junk food and cigarettes. They made ole Frank nervous just by being black and young."

Ellis grimaced and shook his head in wonder but said nothing. Carlton continued.

"I called to let you know that Eleanor and I had a long talk after supper. I've agreed to retire at the end of next month."

Ellis took in a deep breath and let it out as Carlton waited for his reaction.

"Best news I've had in a long time – for you and for Eleanor. Are we still on for the morning."

"I'll be there."

The call ended without another word being exchanged.[55]

Beatrice Huff was baffled to see Carlton come in her diner and head over to Ellis's booth. The widower judge being there on a Saturday morning was more of a rule than an exception, but Carlton coming there to meet him... 'Somethin' must be goin' on,' she thought.

As Carlton slid in across from Ellis, Beatrice set a cup of steaming coffee in front of him and offered Ellis a touch up on his. He smiled and thanked her, adding, "Yes, that would be nice, Beatrice."

She smiled back, took Carlton's order – egg-in-a-hole with a glass of milk – and departed with none of the usual repartee.

Ellis leaned toward Carlton, looked him squarely in the eye and said, "You've done the right thing. You know that don't you?"

"Yeah. It's not easy, but I'm not second-guessin' the decision if that's what's on your mind."

"Good. How did Eleanor react?"

"She teared up, hugged me, and thanked me. It made me realize I should have done this a few years ago."

"What comes next?"

"I'll tell the Mayor. And my policemen. Otherwise, I'll just low-key it."

"Same way I did my retirement, Carlton. I'm proud of you. You won't regret this, and Eleanor will have such a load of worry taken off her shoulders. I'm really proud of you."

"You're repeating yourself, Your Honor."

Ellis laughed. "Guess I am."

Breakfast came, and they idly chatted about retirement's pros and cons until Carlton abruptly changed the subject.

"If you don't mind, I'd like you to indulge me in talking more about policing all these years. I worry that I haven't been the kind of policeman I set out to be."

Ellis thought a few seconds before replying.

"How about the area of race relations?"

"That's exactly the area I'm worried about," Carlton replied.

Ellis took the conversation just where he'd hoped it would go.

"I know you had that situation after you became Chief here that was close to being a serious civil rights disturbance. Tell me about all that again, will you?"

Carlton nodded and took a sip of coffee to collect his thoughts.

"I'll never forget that, Judge. It got started when one my policemen was patrolling on a Saturday afternoon – about this same time of year, in fact. He went to lock up a fella. And, what happened next is the closest to us having a real riot in Union Point. The man had given my policeman trouble, and he had to mace 'im. And there were bystanders there watching."

"And, they didn't like what they saw ..."

"Hold on there, Judge. Just let me keep goin'. So, my policeman brought in this fellow and locked him up and then he went back to where he arrested him. When he got there another fella started to argue with him and they nearly got in a fight. My policeman grabbed him and snatched him over a fence. But, then, he let him go – I don't know why he didn't lock him up. So, he came on back down to City Hall."

"I guess that guy didn't appreciate being thrown over a fence," Ellis offered.

"Can't blame him myself, I suppose," agreed Carlton. "I'd been off that afternoon and when I came back in uniform, down there at city hall there were about 250 blacks, and my policeman was in trouble. When I drove up, I looked over and here comes two state troopers in their cars. They come sliding up in there and jumping out of the cars with their shotguns."

"Not good," interrupted Ellis. Carlton ignored him.

"I drove on up, got out of my car and said, 'What in the world is going on here?' Then everybody wanted to tell me – all at once. My policeman said, 'Ole so-and-so...' Someone else said, 'Your policeman turned against me.' This other black man named Raymond said, 'You know what your policeman did?' Each one tried to tell me different."

"I said, 'Wait a minute, wait a minute. I don't want to hear a durn thing today.' Somebody then said, 'Well, let me...' I said, 'I don't want to hear it, go on home. I don't want to hear nothin' from either side. Go on home.'"

"They were ready to start trouble, and I told the state troopers, 'Get in your cars and drive on off. I don't need y'all.' I said, 'Go on home.' They tried to talk, but I wouldn't let 'em tell me nothin'. I told Raymond, I said, 'I'll see you next week.'"

Ellis was about to raise a question, but thought better of it.

"Monday night, I called each one of my policemen. I told them, 'Now look here, one of our policemen done something wrong.' I said, 'If you were in this situation what would you have done?' I made every one of them tell me what he would have done. I said, 'He handled it wrong. He didn't have no business going back up there picking on that fella. He shouldn't have and if the man said anything to him he shouldn't have done anything unless he had a right to lock the man up. If you got a right to lock him up, lock him up. Don't play with him. Lock him up! If you ever tell a man he's under arrest, lock 'im up.'"

"After I got the police straightened out, I went over to talk to Raymond and told him the same thing. I said, 'Now you were wrong Raymond, you didn't have no business interfering.' He said, 'Well, Chief, they were trying to...' I said, 'You should have told me. You shouldn't have got after him and tried to put on a show like that,' I said, 'You were wrong. Both of y'all were wrong. My policeman was wrong. That's where I want us to drop it, like it is.' I told him, 'Don't ever interfere no more when a policeman is making an arrest. If you got any gripes, you come tell me after and we'll get things straightened out.'"

"We were just that much from havin' a big row. That's how these things get started."

Ellis knew that episode was truly a close call. Fortunately for everyone, Carlton had been able to deflect it with his fairness, force of personality, and promise to hear everyone out after things cooled down. He wondered how many small-town police chiefs would have told the troopers to leave under the circumstances. That must have made a big impression on the demonstrators. The fact that Raymond was open to hearing what Carlton had to say was no small contribution to the good outcome.

"One more question along these lines, Carlton..."

"Fire away, Judge."

"Have you treated blacks any differently from whites all these years?"

Carlton shrugged and then answered in a way that Ellis saw as reflecting his heritage.

"I believe that for a black man, you've got to be firm with him. You got to be fair with him. But, when he's committed a crime, he knows he's got to be punished. He knows that. Put a man in jail when he's committed a crime. Then if you want to help him, you do what you can. Get him in jail first, because that's what the law demands, and then try to get him out."

"If he hasn't done anything bad, then I'll go to court and testify that he just got wild for the day or something like that. And, I'll do my best to try to help him. And, they respect and understand that. When they've committed a crime, they know they got to be punished. They might cuss you out at the time when they are full of liquor. But they appreciate it in the long run."

"I honestly believe that's that same way I'd treat a white man. And, I've tried to teach this to all those new policemen I trained."

Ellis took note of Carlton's use of "they" when talking about black people. The "us" and "them" separateness was inevitably imbued in Carlton through his upbringing. Unlike many though, that separateness had not led Carlton to treat blacks with a lesser justice than whites. Had he done so, Carlton could have been a very different policeman – maybe a rural version of Alabama's Bull Conner.[56]

Then, Ellis remembered a particularly revealing incident Carlton once told him.

"Say, Carlton, didn't you tell me way back when that a black woman drove into your filling station and asked to use your bath room? Does that ring a bell?"

"Why I hadn't thought about that in years. That was way back in the 50s. It was a Saturday afternoon. I know that because that's when a lot of the boys would come over and shoot the breeze all afternoon and into the evenin'. Some would leave but others would show up, so we always had half a dozen or so to liven up the place."

Ellis just nodded his understanding.

"Anyway, we were all sittin' there and this shiny, late-model car come sliding in and stopped in front of us. The driver got out and walked over to me. She could tell I was the owner or manager due to the shirt I was wearin'. Oh, and she was a black lady, and she looked a little nervous and uncomfortable about somethin' or other. So, I said, 'Can I help you?'"

"'Sir, do you have a colored restroom?'"

"I could feel a dozen eyeballs on me from the boys at this point waitin' to see what I'd tell her." Without hesitatin', I told her, 'No, ma'am, we don't, but you are welcome to the one ladies room we have right over there.' And, so she did. A few minutes later she came back out, stopped in front of me and said, 'Thank you, Sir." Then she drove on off. She wasn't there no more than five or six minutes."

Ellis cleared his throat and looked intently at Carlton.

"Did any of your buddies there ask you about why you let her use your restroom?" Ellis asked, "Or say anything when she left?"

"Nope, not a peep from anybody, but I was pretty sure what they were thinking. I could see a couple of them glancing at each other.

"And, what was it they were thinking, Carlton?"

"Why didn't ole Carlton send her down the road to another place. Make it their problem?"

"Why didn't you do just that – send her down the road. You know that's what each one of those men would have done."

"That's not me, Judge. All this stuff about separate rest rooms and so forth just isn't what I got out of my Sunday school lessons."

Ellis had heard enough. The sum total of these various episodes from Carlton's life were more than enough to confirm what Ellis had known for years about Carlton. And, so, he told this to his friend.

"You were and remain a good policeman, Carlton, and you've been fair to all of us here in this county. You have no need to concern yourself that you haven't treated our black fellow citizens fairly."

"Thank you, Ellis. I know you always shoot the truth at me, so your opinion relieves my mind on that subject. I'm grateful to you for the time we've spent together the last couple of days."

"Me, too, Carlton."

There must have been a broad spectrum among the policeman in the South with Connor at the racist extremum. Fortunately for all citizens of Greene County, Carlton Lewis likely fell near the opposite end of this distribution from the Bull Conners. Similarly, most of the leaders above Carlton would not have encouraged or even tolerated racist behavior had Carlton been of Conner's ilk. In many ways, Greene County was blessed with circumstances and leadership that, in the final analysis, resulted in a fairness that let Greene make it through the 60s and 70s without much racial strife.

Because Johnny Grimes, who lived in the historic little community of Penfield[57] as a kid, grew up in the black schools of the county and became Greene's first black sheriff's deputy, he has a special perspective on race relations in those days. When asked why he thought his home county avoided the strife that manifested elsewhere in the South, he would point out a few key factors. The first was that Greene County was a rural farm community with no dense concentrations of people. Houses were spread out and most folks kept to themselves. Life centered around family, schools, and churches.

He also acknowledges Eli Jackson as a key figure at the time in black education. "Professor" Jackson, as he was widely known, was principal of Floyd T. Corry High School. A 2016 posting on the Facebook page *Unearthing Greene County, Georgia African American*, left this tribute: "The late Professor Eli Jackson served our community with eloquence, confidence, determination, perseverance, and a powerful love for each student who came through the hallways of the former Floyd Thomas Corry High School. We honor and celebrate the life and legacy of the late Professor Eli Jackson." The photo accompanying this post shows the Professor seated at a desk while two young black men, both in white shirt and necktie, interact with him. Another post cites "his famous quote 'manners will carry you where money can't.'"

Sheriff Wyatt is also considered by Johnny Grimes as a factor in the peacefulness of Greene's race relations. Grimes explained, "Sheriff Wyatt carried a very big stick in Greene County – he was a fair man, very mild spoken, people respected him and he kept things in hand." Johnny's father had a liquor still, and Sheriff Wyatt caught him a few times. He always brought him home and told him, "Robert, you got too many children for this. You need to stop making whiskey." Wyatt would bring a man before the judge and say, "This man's got six or seven kids at home, it ain't goin' to prove nothin' sendin' him to prison." This approach to compassionate justice resonated with Carlton who shared Grimes' regard for L. L. Wyatt.

There is one major difference, though, between L. L. and

Carlton. L. L. Wyatt killed more than half a dozen men – oddly, the exact number seems hard to determine. Carlton Lewis killed none. His sparing of Charlie Monfort even puzzled a judge in court.

Was Carlton Lewis a good and fair man as Ellis Buchanan judged him to be? Carlton entered the world as grandson to a slave owner and grew up in the Jim Crow era where blacks and whites were segregated in all social aspects. Few whites immersed from birth in such an environment could avoid a life of prejudice. But, one does not have to act on it. Why would someone see a black man and put the emphasis on 'man' while another focuses on 'black?' Most have no answer for that other than it somehow comes from within.

At his funeral, Rev. Hampton asserted that Carlton was "one of the finest Christion men" he knew. Carlton was not merely a church-goer, he took Christian principles to heart and lived his daily life by them. Sure, he was a rough and tumble man who went looking for trouble more than most policemen then or now would, and he tossed a lot of black men in jail. But, he sought justice and fairness for them, sometimes carrying it out on his own initiative.

The black community recognized and appreciated his fairness. They respected him sufficiently to cooperate in defusing a near riot in Union Point. They responded positively to Carlton's efforts in support of his son Tom's political campaigning in Greene, and many would have liked to see Carlton succeed Wyatt as their Sheriff.

Carlton Lewis was a man who loved life, his family, and his God. His religious values guided his daily actions. This was apparent to his community who benefitted from his love of his fellow human beings, regardless of their skin color. Fundamentally, he was a good man – a Christian man – who conducted himself proactively in accordance with Matthew's and Luke's statements of The Golden Rule.

THE END

Harold A. (Hal) McAlister is Regents' Professor Emeritus of Astronomy at Georgia State University and founder and Director Emeritus of the Center for High Angular Resolution Astronomy (CHARA) at GSU. Under his leadership, CHARA designed, built, and now operates the world's highest-resolution telescope. The facility is located on the grounds of the historic Mount Wilson Observatory in the San Gabriel Mountains of Southern California where Edwin Hubble measured the rate of expansion of the Universe in the 1920s using Mount Wilson's 100-inch telescope. From 2002 until 2014, McAlister also served as Director of Mount Wilson Observatory.

Hal was honored by his alma mater, the University of Tennessee at Chattanooga, as its commencement speaker in 2001 and its Distinguished Alumnus in 2008. Graduating with a BA in physics in 1971, he went on to the University of Virginia where he received MA and PhD degrees in astronomy. For the next two years, he was a postdoc at Kitt Peak National Observatory in Tucson, Arizona, where he perfected the high-resolution imaging technique of speckle interferometry for the study of binary stars, of which he discovered some 200. In 1977, he joined the physics and astronomy faculty at Georgia State University from which he retired in 2015.

The author or co-author of more than 300 scientific papers, Hal has also written articles for the non-scientist in addition to editing several conference proceedings. During the 2009 Station Fire, the largest wildfire in Los Angeles County history, his blog attracted several hundred thousand hits while the fire threatened to destroy Mount Wilson Observatory for nearly a month. His reports during the fire crisis were compiled in the 2010 book *Diary of a Fire*. His novel *Sunward Passage* was started in order to pass time sitting on airplanes flying from his home base in Atlanta to Los Angeles. His current book projects include: *Mount Wilson Observatory: A Self-Guided Walking Tour*, *The Unfolding Universe: Karel Hujer's Reflections on the Cosmos*, and *Seeing the Unseen: Mount Wilson's Role in High Angular Resolution Astronomy*.

He and his wife Susan both grew up in Chattanooga, where they met in college, and live in Decatur, Georgia when they are not off visiting their daughter Merritt in Gainesville, Florida or exploring in their motorhome.

Thomas C. (Tom) Lewis is Senior Advisor to the President at Georgia State University where he provides leadership and direction in the areas of government and corporate relations, and serves as the university liaison to federal, state and local governments. Tom has led Georgia State to new levels of public awareness by directing a comprehensive effort to remake the university's identity and communicate its unique urban mission. In his twenty-eight years as Vice President, Senior Vice President, and Senior Advisor to the President, he has advanced the university's legislative agenda, strengthened relations with alumni, and worked to improve Georgia State's internal and external communications.

Tom came to Georgia State in 1991 from the Office of Governor Joe Frank Harris, where he served as Chief of Staff. He has also served the State of Georgia as member and Chairman of the Board for the Jekyll Island Authority. He is currently chairman of the Georgia Chartered Schools Commission and the Georgia Chartered Schools Commission Foundation.

Tom is a former participant of Leadership Georgia and the Etowah Foundation. He is on the Board of Directors of the Georgia Chamber of Commerce, Century Bank of Georgia, and the Rollins Child Development Center, Zell Miller Institute, and is currently Chairman of the State Charter School Commission. Tom has served as a mentor to students at Georgia College and State University through the Georgia Education Mentorship Program. He is a member of the Faith United Methodist Church in Cartersville, Georgia.

Prior to joining the governor's staff, Tom served as President of the Cartersville-Bartow County Chamber of Commerce (1978-1983), where he guided economic development during a critical period of the county's growth; and executive director of the Georgia Franchise Practices Commission (1974-1978), where he developed new standards to regulate this fast-growing industry.

Tom and his wife Patty have three children and five grandchildren.

Endnotes

1 Derwin and Charlie Young were given speedy trials in Greene County Superior Court. Both were convicted of armed robbery and robbery by intimidation for which they got life in prison on the first charge and 20 years for the second. Additionally, Charlie had been charged with malice murder for which he was sentenced to death. Derwin was released from prison in 1986, but Charlie's continued path through the justice system would be more complicated. Charlie spent six years on death row at Georgia's maximum-security prison in Reidsville while the appeal process went forward. In 1982, the U.S. Eleventh Circuit Court of Appeals reversed a federal district court's earlier denial of a writ of habeas corpus to the death sentencing phase on the basis of incompetent representation during trial. Subsequent appeals progressed through the system all the way to the U.S. Supreme Court with the result that double jeopardy prevented Charlie from a second capital punishment trial. While he avoided death, the other two sentences remained in place. Charlie served his time as a model prisoner, spoke to groups of young people, became a Christian and sought forgiveness, and, on one occasion, turned over shotgun shells he found on the prison grounds to guards.

In December 2003, after spending half of his 56 years in prison, Charlie Young was released as a result of a 3-2 vote at his parole hearing. Reuben would have been 75 that year had his life not been taken 28 years earlier.

See: decision on Young v. Zant rendered by the U.S. Court of Appeals for the Eleventh Circuit, Case No. 81-7123 published in the *Federal Reporter* and accessible at https://openjurist.org/677/f2d/792/young-v-zant and Young v. Kemp, Case No. 84-8408 at https://openjurist.org/760/f2d/1097/young-v-kemp-and-h; articles published in *The Atlanta Journal-Constitution*: "Paroled Killer Lives to Serve," by Carlos Campos, June 26, 2004 and "Savage Killer Walks Out on Parole," available at http://alt.prisons. narkive.com/bUNgU2G7/savage-killer-walks-out-on-parole; Associated Press article "Convicted Murderer to be Paroled 28 Years after Death Sentence," which appeared in the October 20, 2003 issue of *The Augusta Chronicle*.

2 Not to be confused with the fictionalized version of Sparta, Mississippi that formed the backdrop for the film and subsequent television series *In the Heat of the Night*.

3 Thomas and Pearl are buried in Powelton Community Cemetery in Hancock County about 13 miles northeast of Sparta on GA-22. Their birth and death dates are from their headstones.

4 Marriage year is from the 1900 U.S. Census enumeration. Other dates in the paragraphs below are also from census data accessed through Ancestry.com unless otherwise noted.

5 Muster Roll of Company B, 55th Regiment, Georgia Volunteer Infantry, Army of Tennessee, C.S.A., Greene County, GA, Stocks Volunteers available at http://www. researchonline.net/gacw/rosters/55infb.htm.

6 From the 1860 U.S. Federal Census Slave Schedules for Hancock as owned by "Wm Lewis." Another Hancock County Lewis – David W. Lewis, a prominent Georgian unrelated to the subject family of this book – owned 76 slaves. The entire county had 8,137 slaves, just over twice its 3,871 free white citizens. For a detailed analysis of such data, see the Georgia State University doctoral dissertation "Upcountry Yeomanry in Antebellum Georgia: A Comparative Analysis," by Terrence Kersey, 2017 available at https://scholarworks. gsu.edu/ history_diss/63/.

7 Muster Roll of Company B, op. cit.

8 William and Mary Lewis are buried in Powelton Community Cemetery in Hancock County about 13 miles northeast of Sparta on GA-22. Their birth and death dates are from their tombstones.

9 From U.S. Department of Veterans Affairs BIRLS Death File, 1850-2010, Accessed through Ancestry.com.

10 Based on information from Carlton Lewis as recorded in the 1986 audio interview of him and on the Wikipedia entry for "USS Anzio (CVE-57)."

11 For an excellent Wyatt biography, see *The High Sheriff of Greene: The True Story of Legendary Lawman L. L. Wyatt*, by Claire Underwood Hertzler, Deed Publishing: Athens, GA, 2016, 144 pages.

12 Extracted from Vietnam War U.S. Military Fatal Casualty Statistics, National Archives at https://www.archives.gov/research/military/vietnam-war/casualty-lists/state-level-alpha.html.

13 There are any number of on-line and written biographies of Connor, and a particularly interesting one is *The Bull Falls Twice: The Life of Eugene "Bull" Connor*, Judge Tennant M. Shallwood, Jr., Friesans Book Manufacturing, 2001, 166 page.

14 Chain gangs were a 1908 Georgia innovation, and the practice spread throughout the country but was especially popular in the South. While they were mostly comprised of black prisoners, poor whites were also given labor sentences. Employing gangs in badly needed road work was

advocated as a valuable service that few wanted to perform and put prisoners out in the sunlight and fresh air rather than keeping them locked up in cells. After the War, public reaction to seeing a group of men on the roads connected by long leg and waist chains grew increasingly negative. Cruelty was commonly practiced by the guards on their charges who worked from sunup to sundown. The practice generally ended before World War II except for Georgia where it continued until 1945 when Governor Ellis Arnall included its abolition in a reform of the state's prison system. Although chain gangs for state felons are gone, many Georgia counties continued the use of prisoner labor through special work camps, some of which persist to this very day. See: *Chain Gangs, Roads, and Reform in North Carolina, 1900-1935*, PhD dissertation by Susan W. Thomas, UNC Greensboro, 2011; *Chain Gangs*, Other Free Encyclopedia at http:// encyclopedia.jrank.org/articles/pages/6045/Chain-Gangs.html.

15 The author first saw this expression in books by the great mystery writer James Lee Burke, but it is likely not original to him.

16 Today, you would also risk exposure to Hep B and C, HIV, and Herpes.

17 The main state prison of the Georgia Department of Corrections – Georgia State Prison – is located at Reidsville in Tatnell County about 150 miles southeast of Greensboro, close to Vidalia with its famous onions. Until 1980, the state's death row was situated there prior to being relocated to Jackson in Butts County at the Georgia Diagnostic and Classification State Prison. The Reidsville facility houses approximately 1550 inmates. Nearby is the Rogers State Prison, a medium-security prison farm facility.

18 This person's name has been changed to protect privacy.

19 Williams' driving record was noted by many news outlets in his later years at and at his death, e.g. in *The New York Times* at https://www.nytimes.com/2000/ 11/17/us/hosea-williams-74-rights-crusader-dies.html and *The Los Angeles Times* at http://articles. latimes.com/1991-09-01/news/mn-2345_1_hosea-williams.

20 The "Civil Rights Movement Veterans" is an outstanding resource for the history its title implies. The Crawfordville-Taliaferro County events are described there in detail at http://www.crmvet.org/tim/tim65b.htm#1965crawford.

21 ibid., see quote by Frances Pauley, then Director of the Georgia Council on Human relations.

22 Among the many reports of this history, e.g. Williams' obituary in *The*

Guardian, Sunday, November 19, 2000 at
https://www.theguardian.com/news/2000/nov/20/guardian
obituaries.haroldjackson.

23 This history of the Forsyth marches is from
http://www.aboutnorthgeorgia.com/
ang/Civil_Rights_March,_January,_1987.

24 The Southern Poverty Law Center subsequently filed a suit against the
Klansmen involved in the attack, winning a $1M judgement against them.
Williams decided to withdraw from the lawsuit and urged other plaintiffs
to do the same. *The Los Angeles Times* reported on October 26, 1988 that
"Williams, a veteran civil rights activist and King's 'field general' during
the 1960s, said last week that he decided to drop out of the case because he
did not want to impoverish working-class klan members. He urged others
to follow his example. 'You have the choice of joining me in following the
teachings of Christ and Martin Luther King Jr. by forgiving our white
brothers and sisters in Forsyth County,' Williams wrote in a letter to the
remaining plaintiffs. 'Or the choice of participating in the taking of their
homes, their cars, their paychecks, further entrenching racial hatred . . . .'"

25 This episode was related to the author by Tom Lewis.

26 From a 2016 analysis by the National Law Enforcement Officers Memorial
Fund of Department of Justice data. See https://thinkprogress.org/new-
report-on-police-deaths-comes-with-grim-revelations-516b20b0dff7/.

27 See "Inside Central State Hospital, once the world's largest mental
institution," *Atlanta Magazine,* February 2015 issue, available at
http://www.atlantamagazine. com/great-reads/asylum-inside-central-
state-hospital-worlds-largest-mental-institution/.

28 Based upon a story related by Johnny Grimes with the subject individual's
name changed for privacy.

29 ibid.

30 As related by Carlton Lewis in 1986 with the person's actual name altered.

31 See "Union Point Chief," *The Atlanta Constitution,* January 28, 1974, p.
22.

32 Hertzler, op. cit., p. 117.

33 "New Era, New Problems for South's Sheriffs," by William E. Schmidt, *The
New York Times,* September 10, 1984, p. A1.

34 See *The Atlanta Constitution,* December 20, 1981, p. 87.

35 Details from the arrest and trial are from reports in *The Herald-Journal* on October 24, 1975, and subsequent articles in Tom Lewis's clippings from his father's career years.

36 As recalled in the interview with Mary Finch.

37 The SEC complaint against Stewart and his finance companies is available at https://www.sec.gov/litigation/litreleases/lr18141.htm.

38 See "Georgia Mayor Commits Suicide," *UPI Archives*, 13 May 2004 at https://www.upi.com/Archives/2004/05/13/Georgia-mayor-commitssuicide/ 3461084420800/.

39 See "How Two Women Helped Unravel a Lending Empire," by Carrick Mollenkamp, *Wall Street Journal*, 11 Nov 2004 at https://www.wsj.com/articles/SB110012290920070532 and "A Town Betrayed," by Jaime Holguin, *CBS News*, reported on 6 Dec 2004 at https://www.cbsnews.com/news/a-town-betrayed/.

40 See Wikipedia entry for J. B. Stoner at https://en.wikipedia.org/wiki/J._B._Stoner.

41 See "GA US Senate – D Primary" at "Our Campaigns" website https://www. ourcampaigns.com/RaceDetail.html?RaceID=236090 for details of that election.

42 See "Georgia Gubernatorial Election, 1982" at https://en.wikipedia.org/wiki/ Georgia_ gubernatorial_election,_1982.

43 These details are from the written decision of the Eleventh Circuit when Wallace's appeal was heard by them on September 30, 1981. See "Wallace v. State," 37517, Supreme Court of Georgia Decisions.

44 See "Prowl Call Nabs Suspected Killer," *The Atlanta Constitution*, May 18, 1979, p. A1.

45 See "Man Indicted in Officer's Killing," *The Atlanta Constitution*, July 24, 1979, p. 24; "Police-Slaying Trial Postponed," *The Atlanta Constitution*, July 25, 1979, p. 30.

46 See "Jury Selection Begins in Murder Trial," *The Atlanta Constitution*, February 14, 1980, p. 5.

47 See: "Defense Rests Case in Police Slaying," *The Atlanta Constitution*, February 15,1980, p. 53; "Washington Man Convicted," *The Atlanta Constitution*, February 16, 1980, p. 3; and, "Wallace v. State," 37517, Supreme Court of Georgia Decisions, Decided September 30, 1981.

48 See "Court Throws Out Murder Conviction," *The Atlanta Constitution*,

March 14, 1985, p. 30.

49 See "Judge Rejects Death Verdict Because of DA's Statement," *The Atlanta Constitution*, March 9, 1985, p. 30; "Wallace v. Kemp," U.S. Court of Appeals, Eleventh Circuit Decisions, No. 84-8297, Decided

March 13, 1985; "In Second Trial, Defendant Cleared in Officer's Slaying," *The Atlanta Constitution*, June 5, 1987, p. 41; "Mental State Not Issue as Man Cleared," *The Atlanta Constitution*, June 6, 1987, p. 29; "Habeas Corpus Writ Filed," *The Atlanta Constitution*, June 12, 1987, p. 15; "Man Who Did Face Execution Released," *The Atlanta Constitution*, June 18, 1987, p. 97; "Robert Wallace," *The National Registry of Exonerations Pre-1989*, at https://www.law.umich.edu/special/exoneration/Pages/casedetailpre1989.aspx?caseid=352

50 Now Georgia College, the state's designated public liberal arts university.

51 Claude and Addie Jones are both buried in Norwood Cemetery in Warren County. See https://www.findagrave.com/memorial/121222246/claude-a.-jones.

52 *The Living Constitution*, by David A. Strauss, Oxford Univ. Press, 2010, pp. 126-132.

53 This brief overview of Southern Reconstruction is informed by articles in the online *Encyclopedia Britannica* entitled "Reconstruction," "Andrew Johnson, " and "Jim Crow Law."

54 See *Hiring the Black Worker: The Racial Integration of the Southern Textile Industry, 1960-1980,* by Timothy Minchin, (UNC Press), 1999. See review at https:// eh.net/book_reviews/hiring-the-black-worker-the-racial-integration-of-the-southern-textile-industry-1960-1980/.

55 Carlton retired on March 1, 1986. It was announced in the Valentine's Day issue of *The Herald-Journal* in an article that also carried a letter from Carlton to the residents of Union Point. Toward the end of that letter, he wrote, "While February 28th will officially be my last day as Police chief of Union Point, it will not be my last day of being involved in many of our County's positive programs. I do intend to stay active and participate wherever I can." As described in this book, a dinner was held in his honor on Wednesday, March 5, 1986, and he died ten days later.

56 The archetypal brutal Southern policeman was Theophilus Eugene Conner, a name more readily recognized as "Bull" Connor. Connor was Birmingham, Alabama's elected Commissioner of Public Safety for a quarter century. Admired by many and reviled by many more for his

behavior towards those attempting to end the Jim Crow racism that had been hardwired for generations into much of Southern life. His tactics famously included the use of dogs and firehoses to disperse demonstrators. Even more sinister was his practice of giving racist counter demonstrators some unhindered time with marchers disembarking their buses before the police would intervene.

During an early 1963 demonstration in a city park by Birmingham students whose ages were between 6 and 18, Connor ordered in the dogs. He was quoted as saying "I want to see the dogs work. I want to see the niggers run." He then let loose the fire hoses on the children who had just been attacked by dogs. Photographs of all this galvanized Americans, most significantly President Kennedy who thereafter addressed civil rights head-on until his death. Lyndon Johnson then saw to it that Kennedy's wishes were realized in the Civil Rights Act of 1964.

57 Penfield was founded in 1829 and became the first home of Mercer University, which relocated to Macon following the Civil War. The Penfield Historic District, comprising more than 300 acres, is on the National Register of Historic Places. Johnny Grimes considered Penfield to be a "great place to raise kids."

95323131R00109

Made in the USA
Lexington, KY
07 August 2018